Edited by
Ekaterina Degot
and
David Riff

The Way Out of . . .

HATJE
CANTZ

Contents

Appendix

Introduction

Ekaterina
Degot and
David Riff

In his essay for this volume, artist Hiwa K poignantly describes something that might be familiar to many a reader: a deep disappointment in art—not only in the system of Western art, but his own practice as well. A glut of political art in public space over the last forty years has done nothing to stop the rise of neoliberalism, heightening the division between rich and poor, he rightly notes, emphasizing that even the biggest exhibition in the world barely reaches 800,000 people, while a Trump speech reaches billions. Determined to do something less purely symbolic, he recently returned to Kurdistan, calling himself a failed political artist, to find a way out. "I realized that we need nurses more than partisans. The time of partisans is over, even of artists. To cure, to midwife, to nurse, that's more important for me," he writes, going on to describe his inspiring efforts to create a local practice that truly changes the lives of its participants.

Hiwa K represents a particularly courageous case of an artist finding a way out of the Western art world, but his is by no means the only departure from the institutional frame or the ideological enclosure that makes up our field. Today, more than ever, these frames seem highly suspect, and certainly not only because of a pause in exhibitions and conferences due to the COVID-19 pandemic. Our art world seems untenable in its elitism and unsustainable in its environmental impact, embroiled in a deep crisis that can only be understood as something with many different causes and articulations. One could call it a polycrisis or simply a perfect storm.

The search for an exit from these multiple crises was one of the intentions behind *The Way Out*, the ambitious but ambivalent title given to the 2021 edition of the interdisciplinary festival steirischer herbst. Referring to the outdoor character of many works, as well as to the desire to break out of the current impasse in the arts, the festival tentatively suggested how art might reconnect with its audiences and face challenges environmental as well as political, old as well as new, that are deeply rooted in its inherent contradictions as well as imposed by the capitalist world order. The catalogue of this festival edition, with a collection of scripts and artists' texts featured in art projects, is being published in parallel with the present volume. Its name, more concretely, is *The Way Out of…*, and it features texts by contributors to the festival's discussion program, with some additions. In this anthology of essays, contributors look more closely at some of the crises society faces today. Each searches for ways out of intractable problems that have been long in coming, but are now becoming as urgent as ever.

Most immediately, the pandemic clearly showed that even the most well-reputed health care systems in the world would buckle under the strain of daily admissions and intensive-care cases. Never has the care crisis seemed so urgent. In her essay, sociologist and historian Emma Dowling unpacks the definitions and ideologies of care to look at the causes of why health care systems burn out: behind the fetishization of self-care we can find arguments for cost efficiency producing a need for underpaid and unpaid labor. The way out of the crisis, Dowling maintains, not only lies in allocating more time, money, and societal capacities; it also involves the democratization of care through the bottom-up reorganization of its institutions, but also urgently requires facilitation and adequate pay for home care through relatives. "Reversing the trend toward privatizing and individualizing the responsibility and the cost of care is not simply a moral imperative; it can also help to devise more effective and efficient forms of care that are more integrated across everyday life," she argues.

It was already clear long before the pandemic that digital communication has fundamentally altered the very nature of the economy. A profound transformation of digital infrastructures is underway, media theorist and historian Evgeny Morozov argues, yet we are unable to imagine anything better than a "surveillance capitalism." In his talk for steirischer herbst '21, reproduced here, Morozov criticizes the left's inability to formulate a program beyond the democratization of data ownership, or the breakup of Big Tech monopolies, and asks what alternatives there might be. Morozov sees potential in using AI and "smart cities" to reactivate socialist planning, but argues that it is also important to think beyond basic needs in inventing new forms of socialist digitization, and maybe also learn from a neoliberal thinker like Friedrich Hayek, who believed in the market's self-regulatory capacities as a basis for personal freedom. Morozov proposes that we draw strength from this admittedly by-now utopian-sounding idea. The boundary between work and play, necessity and freedom should be eroded in an alternative vision of digitization: "Instead of building a socialist society which further entrenches the division between work and play, necessity and freedom, we should be building a system where value is produced as we go about living our lives, whether it involves repairing broken washing machines or learning languages or writing essays."

Today, the notion of "self-regulatory markets" has a utopian potential never fulfilled by a neoliberal order. Instead, over recent years, such unequal globalism has prompted an ever more desperate national response. Is there any way out of this kind of harmful globalism that doesn't entail a return to national and parochial tradition? In pursuit of this question,

OUT 15

historian Quinn Slobodian queries two contrasting
mid-20th-century thinkers who each found his way
to alternative political geographies that were neither
global nor national. One is Karl Polanyi, a left-liberal
critic of neoliberalism avant la lettre. The other,
perhaps somewhat unexpectedly, is the juridical
and political philosopher Carl Schmitt, a Catholic
Nazi and lifelong conservative. As much as they
were otherwise at odds, their major commonality,
according to Slobodian, was that they saw the US as
the prime representative of a market and a state out
of control, metaphorically understood as a golem,
robot, or Leviathan. Interestingly, both arrived at two
different versions of regionalist thinking, in which
autarkic regions opt out of global interconnection.
Slobodian does not endorse this vision, but leaves
us with a haunting question: "What ways out of
globalism can we find that don't rely on the fiction
of regional autarky or the comic-book villain of a
man-machine made of steel? How can we disagree
with both Polanyi and Schmitt without falling into
the embrace of American universal capitalism?"

Over the last two years, the whole world has
started looking more closely at another side of this
"American universal capitalism," namely, its reliance
upon racialized power relations shaped by centuries
of European colonial domination. The Black Lives
Matter movement has drawn attention to this major
issue, spreading from the US to Europe. But in the
German-speaking countries, so-called critical race
theory is an uneasy fit, Mark Terkessidis points out in
his essay, exploring the historical reasons for why the
Black and White color scheme does not necessarily
work in Central Europe.

To get beyond an uncritical use of theories and
practices imported from the US, Central Europeans
must look at the real histories of domination, exclusion, and exploitation at work in this postimperial

space, Terkessidis argues. For the German-speaking world, Eastern and Southern Europe are former colonial zones whose inhabitants were once barely fit to serve as "guest workers"—a term that originated from none other than Joseph Goebbels. As Terkessidis argues, it is high time to confront these ghosts of the past and their contradictions. "Considering this history, it seems wrong to omit certain experiences from the increasingly generalized schematic of 'white' and Black. The transferal of models from the US currently seems like a textbook escape from a discriminatory society; the real way out, however, would be to look at all experiences of historical injustice and present-day racism within a common frame, without denying their differences," he writes.

A similar example of "showcase politics" could be seen in the way most politicians, companies, and ideologies treat the impending human-made environmental catastrophe, of which COVID-19 might actually be one further articulation. In his essay, Jason W. Moore challenges the basic assumptions underlying mainstream environmentalism, an "eco-industrial complex," as he calls it, which produces little more than "apocalyptic warnings coupled with incrementalist reform." Moore argues that the idea of the ecological collapse as a result of overpopulation and overconsumption has a disturbing link to the thinking of 18th-century economist Thomas Malthus, who blamed all economic and social problems on overpopulation by the poor. Environmentalism since the 1970s has been similarly driven by elitist ideas, unable to link up with other struggles, its planetary thinking "imperial" and informed by a "holism of the rich." This is why it blames humanity at large for breaking the laws of nature, but never names the profit-driven system that creates so many intersecting crises. The way out of

OUT17

this environmentalism involves understanding how "climate class divide, climate patriarchy, and climate apartheid" are interrelated as causes of the current situation and not just effects of the generalized "Anthropocene" and its inevitable collapse, again and again showcased in ineffectual, demonstrative political performances.

If "showcase politics" is a common problem among the multiple crises of our time, this also concerns the question of sexuality and power. Here, too, one could ask whether it is really enough to unmask and cancel exemplary abusers, in the hope that a new codex of fair heterosexual relations will arise around a notion of consent and transparency. "How to conceive of a better sexual world for women?" Katherine Angel asks in her essay. Certainly, in a situation where not only rape and violence but just plain bad sex abound, women need to resist being turned into objects by violent men, Angel argues, including by affirming their own desire, by giving or denying their consent to enter sexual relations. The problem is that desire itself is relational, tricky, and its discussion must acknowledge the actual messiness of sexuality—something that is "rife with contradictions, ambiguity, confusion." Consent can be given, withdrawn, fatally misread, et cetera. Women, says Angel, cannot be expected to solve the problems of pleasure and power singlehandedly. "The injunction to know and express your desire, as a measure to foreclose rape, is a heavy burden to bear." Not only should we be asking "what forms of power are operating in the room," but we should also be asking about how desire really arises, in all of its complexity, and how it becomes a problem.

Paul B. Preciado concurs with this opinion when he writes in his essay, "we have a problem of organization of sensitivity, of structure of desire," pointing to the massive poisoning of the planet and of all relations of people to one another and to themselves. "The dimension of the sex-racial capitalist destruction of life requires a change in the understanding of politics, a deepening of the levels of struggle, a move away from the segmented identity languages that separate and even oppose anti-capitalist, ecological, anti-racist, anti-patriarchal, feminist, queer, and trans struggles to imagine the whole process of systemic mutation (linguistic, cognitive, libidinal, energetic, institutional, relational . . .)," he writes. Nevertheless, he feels, there is cause for optimism. New struggles, as yet in their infancy, assert the subjectivity of a *"somatopolitical Lumpenproletariat,"* those excluded and abused by the current system, created by our own (older) generation, its mistakes, and its compromises. A new generation of activists is emerging to demand a detox, and Preciado joins it eagerly, advising it to embrace its own hybridities and mutations, and not to waste time joining "the dominant sex-racial capitalist binary, and heteropatriarchal culture."

All of the authors collected in *The Way Out of . . .* agree: the current moment is one of multiple crises for which there is no easy solution, requiring structural changes that actually engage with the messy reality out there. Instead of "showcase politics" for the media, a real new awareness is required to make sense of how all the problems and crises of the Capitalocene are connected. But equally clear is that the increasingly desperate situation leaves no other option: a sweeping change is on the horizon and already in its infancy.

This is more than clear in our own field, the world of contemporary art, whose very forms and formats are in doubt. Art has long since been locked into a system of white cubes and black boxes, which earlier cultural vanguards tried to escape, perhaps at the cost of becoming an even more exclusive

club for the knowing. Today, however, there is a
massive change from within the art world, whose
very structures are shifting, as Dorothea von
Hantelmann points out in her text.

Clear evidence for this larger shift is the crossover
between visual and performing arts, and the resulting fusion of two very "different kinds of ritualistic
topologies," both of which are by now possibly
outdated. The black box of theater or performance
forms and organizes small and limited collectives
through the shared time of spectatorship. Museums
speak to the people at large, who can visit during
opening hours to practice looking at objects and
pictures of objects as the valued artifact of productivist, materialist society. Today, such a mode of viewing
appears "too static, too unsocial, and too focused on
the object" to encompass the increasingly relational
and porous space of social interaction, which par-
tially explains the attempts to fuse the museum with
the older limited collectivity of the theater. This might
be a dead end, Hantelmann suggests. A new format
would have to be porous, an "individualized space for
events" not trapped in the institution, but open, also
in terms of time, allowing new forms of connectivity
to emerge. Such formats are indeed already emerging
beyond the white cube and the black box, becoming
increasingly relevant in times when enclosed space
and closed formats no longer work. A good example
would be Hiwa K's performance *Cooking with Mama*,
described in the essay already mentioned above.

Hantelmann notes that one of the reasons why
object-viewer relations of the traditional museum
have reached a dead end is that they rest upon
distance and separation, and not interaction and
immersion. These distances and separations have
only become greater with measures taken to
combat the pandemic, as audiences appear in tightly
organized windows, with masks that act as focusing

blinders. The museum, probably the least crowded institution, has become an even more restrictive and exclusive space than it ever was. In his essay, artist Thomas Hirschhorn argues that we urgently need to start thinking about how to get out of this distanced, separated situation. The way out, as he sees it, lies not only in overcoming the new social distances centimeter by centimeter, but also in moving out of the exclusive institution into public space, where art must and can prove that it is as essential as a shopping mall. To Hirschhorn, a museum should be "a public space, a home, or even a shelter," and would no longer require ideal locations, but rather a new mode of address for the nonexclusive audience. Its founding principles would be presence (of artists and public) and production (together, where artists draw audiences into the work). This is how, finding the way out of its current predicament, art can reimagine its institutions as a Museum of the Future—an accessible, living, open, porous space where audiences not accustomed to art would finally feel that they are treated with respect and kindness, as equal partners. This is how art can also regain its relevance and bring perspectives to society, showing ways out that are better than those currently available to us.

22 THE   WAY

The Way Out of Failed Political Art

Hiwa K

I'm really happy that steirischer herbst invited
me to revive my old project *Cooking with Mama,*
where I called my mom to ask her for recipes. After
sixteen years, it was at the back of my memory,
and also the art world's. Nowadays, it has become
so urgent to call each other because we're so much
more divided. And while the project used to be
about belonging, now it's about longing.

When developing an artwork, I don't have
an initial idea. I start from darkness, slowly, in a
Darwinian way. My projects always teach me along
the way, and this one is still unfolding. The art piece,
for me, is something that doesn't submit to the
control of the artist, but goes further, and always
brings in the voices of other people. For me, this is
its political aspect.

The portable kitchen, in this project, isn't a
message; it's more the medium itself, which creates
possibilities. Sometimes the cooking sessions are
done in a touristic or self-exoticizing way. It's important not to do this. People shouldn't speak only a
certain refined language; we shouldn't be patronizing
as artists and intellectuals. In previous sessions, we
never had viewers, only participants. That was the
most important thing. But of course now, because of
sanitary regulations, we couldn't involve everyone in
the cooking process.

The project started in 2005, when I was pretending
to be a student in an art academy. I was making
projects on the body of the academy as an institution.
I was supposed to be painting. I was supposed to be
making sculptures. But then we had a kitchen in the
academy, and I hadn't seen my mother in four years.
I'd almost forgotten what she looked like. Back then
there were no online things. Someone told me about
Messenger, and I somehow learned how to work
with the app, and then I asked my family to join me,
extending our kitchen from Iraq. I was interested
in how the fatherland or the motherland dissolves
and we become one. It was about how you translate

OUT

organic food into the digital and back into organic food in another country.

During the Occupy Wall Street movement, I couldn't get a visa to go. Instead, we had Occupy Berlin, where we had 300 people protesting for a long time in Prinzessinnengärten. We started a huge kitchen, in which 70 people cooked at the same time for 300 people with big pots and we made very slow food. It took hours.

When the project started, I didn't think that it would extend to other people because I was happy to do it with my mom. After eight or nine years, I realized that we had to stop the project because my mom had run out of recipes. Each time, we had to cook something that I didn't know—that's the point of the project, which makes it dynamic.

When we first extended to others, I was interested in the stories behind the food. For example, one of the people who cooked with his mother was from South Korea, and they made something very traditional from there. But actually, it had become traditional only after the American army had gone from the country and left lots of canned food behind. So, this canned food, American food, was integrated into Korean cuisine. Here, the issue is how you can translate a situation. How much can you learn from your enemies, or so-called enemies? In this case, I don't see war as only a bad thing. This may sound absurd, but sometimes there are some good aspects, some beautiful aspects.

In another session, I had a Kurdish guy from Turkey contact his mother. He grew up in Istanbul and was never allowed to speak Kurdish, and his mom never learned Turkish. So, imagine a son talking to his mother and the sisters having to translate between them. The mother came from a village where they didn't have much access to school. It's easier in villages to refuse to learn Turkish because you don't have the opportunity to learn it. The son only learned Turkish because he had to.

I was always trying to find out about these stories. But even in itself, cooking together and gathering is very important, especially at this moment. I was isolated for many months. Even in Iraq, I didn't have access to my family. I'm talking about a few months ago, last winter. It always brings me to this idea of finding new strategies.

So, what I like about the coronavirus situation is that it highlights the loneliness we were experiencing before this division, with which we've always lived but which we didn't recognize. Coronavirus just pinned it down for us. It put it on the table for us. So that's the good side of it: knowing that we're in danger of being even more separated from each other. This is eye-opening for many, many people.

Being Kurdish, we're divided by four countries, and we're always a minority. Forty million people are considered a minority—what an interesting joke! We have to learn Farsi, we have to learn Arabic, we have to learn Turkish. And additionally, I learned English, German, and Dutch. You somehow adapt the architecture of your mouth when you speak another language; you have a different setting of the tongue and jaw. With food it's the same. When you taste something, it challenges a kind of nationalistic approach or a comfort zone or what you call the food of your childhood. If you compare it to music, at first it sounds a little bit false, but as soon as you play it more often—two or three times—it doesn't sound false anymore.

I recently returned to Kurdistan because I was very disappointed by my own practice and also, in general, by art and Western art. We've had so much art in public space, political art in the last forty years. But at the same time, we see neoliberalism becoming stronger and stronger. Capitalism is occupying more

OUT   27

space, and the division between rich and poor is getting wider and wider. For example, a speech by Trump reaches billions of people in one day, while the biggest exhibition in the world didn't even reach 800,000 people in total.

So, I started to think about this phrase of Muhammad, who says, if you want to resist something or change something, start with your hands. And if you don't have the opportunity, start with your tongue. So first is the hand, which means the revolution, which we can forget about right now. The second is the tongue, which means protest and political art and critique, which we're doing. And if you don't have that opportunity, which we don't have, it remains only symbolic. This is happening in the art world.

The least you can do is go to the heart. It sounds a little romantic, but that's what happens: you slip into the heart. I realized that we need nurses more than partisans. The time of partisans is over, even of artists. To cure, to midwife, to nurse, that's more important for me. And that's why I started to work on a farm taking care of animals and trees, being close to my city and trying to organize group talks together to see what could be done. Sometimes I have a meeting with a group of poets and before they write poems, we say, "Let's go and clean this mountain or this hill of plastic." And while cleaning, everyone writes a poem and then we read them. This connection to the source could be read as an indirect anti-capitalist act, but because it's closer to myself, closer to the heart, it's more political than my other work.

I gave an interview to *Monopol* magazine recently, which was called "Ich bin ein gescheiterter politischer Künstler" (I'm a failed political artist).[1] I don't mean only me. I mean political art itself. It needs to change.

28 THE WA

Some people tell me this sounds like New Age spiritualism. I don't care about that. It's about the urgency of going to the heart and reconnecting there—not about the concept of political art. We talk a lot about collectivity, but, in the end, it's never collective. Collectives always fall apart because there is no real connection. We need different practices, not to make a paradise out of hell, but to make hell less hellish.

I think it was very important for me to go to Kurdistan and to work directly with people. I live somewhere where you don't have rain, and Turkey is depriving the whole country of water because they've built 200 dams. Other countries are in the same situation. When people ask me, "What do you think about Alan Kurdi?"—this small child who drowned in the sea—I say, "Well, we have to talk about people who don't have the luxury to drown at sea. It can be a luxury to drown there. There are people who don't even have the voice to talk about their pain."

The obsession of this art world system is to make stars. I'm not a star; I'm a moon. Even a half moon is enough. As soon as you become a star, you become too far away. I prefer to be a half moon—the moon, but like a neighbor.

OUT 29

1 Hiwa K, "Ich bin ein gescheiterter politischer Künstler," interview by Saskia Trebing, *Monopol*, July 5, 2019, https://www.monopol-magazin.de/ich-bin-ein-gescheiterter-politischer-kuenstler, accessed December 12, 2021.

OUT

32 THE WA

Ways Out of the Care Crisis

Emma
Dowling

OUT 33

Despite the importance of care, caring appears to be attributed very little value by society, at least when measured by the dominant standards of income or social status. While everyone needs a nurturing and caring environment throughout their lives, caring activities are some of the most undervalued and invisible of all, and those who perform them are among the most neglected and unsupported people in our societies. The coronavirus has made it even more difficult to ignore the crisis of care and the consequences of an underresourced health and social care system. It has brought into view the lack of resources and equipment available to health and other care workers, as well as issues of understaffing, long hours, and low pay in the care sector.[1] The tragic inability to sufficiently protect not only the staff but also so many of the residents of care homes is also symptomatic of the lack of value attributed to care recipients.[2] All in all, the desperate shortcomings of a "just-in-time" economy with few reserves have been made evident. Societies that systematically erode their care infrastructures cannot thrive in the long term. Since the beginning of the pandemic, in countries where public infrastructures were absent, threadbare due to austerity, or beholden to the logics of cost efficiency as the basis for profit making, the struggle to contain the pandemic was especially severe. That's because care needs don't go away just because there is no funding for them.

If, after the global financial crisis of 2008, it was big banks that were considered part of a critical infrastructure that was too big to fail, the coronavirus crisis thrust into the limelight all those normally invisible workers who do the work of keeping life and society going day in and day out. This includes all the unpaid labor carried out within the privatized realm of the home. The assumption that all of this work would simply get done somehow reflects an

OUT35

implicit societal reliance on the family and, with
that, women as the fallback unit for care and social
reproduction: during lockdowns, families turned
their homes into offices, nurseries, and schools, with
an uneven burden of the work involved falling on
women. And not everyone was able to find a safe
haven in lockdown, whether that was because they
had to continue traveling to work, because they
were driven out of the home by domestic abuse, or
because they did not have a home in the first place.
Those undertaking care work across the spectrum
of paid and unpaid labor belong to those key or
essential workers on whom society relies. And yet,
there is a contradiction between the importance of
this labor and its systematic devaluation.

~~Care: Definitions~~

But what exactly is care? What does someone mean
when they use the term? A minimal definition would
be that caring means taking responsibility for the
basic needs of another person who is unable to
provide for these needs herself. More broadly, the
physical and emotional labors that make up caring
activities are considered part of a whole host of
reproductive activities that are vital to sustaining
and maintaining life.[3] Indeed, they are the very
condition for the economy to function. However,
congealed in the meaning of care is a limit to
thinking in terms of the economy and productivity
alone, because it is necessary to care for those who
are not or no longer economically productive. Also,
despite the ways in which we might be compelled
to do so, most of us don't think of ourselves simply
as labor power for economic production, and we
don't find it fulfilling to organize our lives simply in
accordance with the demands of our jobs and the
requirements of the labor market—that is indeed a
source of burnout!

 WAY

Professional and much of unpaid care work entails a challenging bundle of tasks. It includes assisting someone with the activities of personal care, which can involve getting up and going to bed, washing, eating, and so forth, and can also include medical procedures. Helping someone with such tasks is not reducible to the physical motions, but can involve the need to motivate the person, soothe them, direct them, reassure them, and respond to social situations that are not predictable or easily routinized. In care work, physical and emotional tasks are intertwined and cannot be neatly separated: caring means listening, observing, interpreting, and making sense of someone's needs; it means interacting, assisting, and understanding. Caring for others involves complex tasks that require sophisticated social and communicative skills, as well as expertise, along with empathetic and intuitive abilities. However, especially in a care system under pressure, it is those very skills and competencies that are either made invisible, seen as simply that which people bring to the job, or externalized due to no longer being considered part of care work's paid dimensions. And while caring can be hard work and involves affects that are not always "nice," caring also means doing something with attention, affection, and concern. The latter not only makes life worth living, but may also very well prolong the cared-for person's life. This qualitative, indeed ethical, dimension of care is also a source of its exploitation: care is exploited because people "care"—because they have a sense of public service, because they have a sense of responsibility, because they have compassion.

~~Care: Ideologies~~

Indeed, we should cast a critical eye on the ideological dimensions of care and caring. Feminists have long been challenging the naturalization of gender and the idea that care work is simply the mobilization of a feminine propensity to care.[4] Across the globe, women still do significantly more unpaid (and paid) care work than men. According to figures from the International Labour Organization, paid care work makes up nearly twenty percent of global female employment and less than seven percent of global male employment; when it comes to unpaid care work, men might today be increasingly involved with childcare at home, but mothers frequently retain the primary responsibility for the overall "management" of childcare and are more likely to be in part-time employment.[5] In Austria, as in other places, the overwhelming majority of adults who need care are tended to in unpaid ways by relatives, the majority of whom are female. Difficulties in reconciling work and care often lead to losses in gainful employment, for example by not taking on much responsibility professionally or by working part-time. Sometimes, gainful employment has to be foregone altogether. Loneliness and lacking time for one's own needs are also common.[6]

In frontline care work in particular, the structural discriminations inscribed in contemporary labor markets are exploited. This means that people with less bargaining power in the labor market—not just women, but also racialized or migrant and cross-border workers—are the ones who find themselves at the receiving end of the devaluation of care. For example, in Austria roughly six percent of the care provided to people in need of support is twenty-four-hour live-in care. This paid care work is mainly done on the basis of a two-week roster system by women from neighboring countries including Slovakia, the Czech Republic, Romania, and Bulgaria. They are often placed by agencies and work self-employed. Their position combines the social devaluation of care and structural discrimination. The border closures and travel restrictions during the pandemic have especially highlighted once again how much people living here depend on these migrant or cross-border care activities.[7] We can see how care deficits in Austria are increasingly being met by female care capacities from other countries with lower wages and more difficult conditions in the labor market.[8] Consequently, it is important to critically interrogate societal discourses of care work and its status, and to ask to whom the role of caring is attributed and on what basis.

A further ideological aspect is brought to the fore by mental-health and disability-rights movements, which have been vocal about the needs, wishes, and desires of care recipients, fighting the stigmatization of disability as well as demanding adequate care. Within disability-rights movements, the narrow focus on care as a purely positive form of affection has been problematized, highlighting not just the unequal distribution of care burdens, but the patron-izing aspects of care within unequal power relations. Disability-rights activists have voiced caution about the "custodial overtones" of care.[9] They have pointed to how, for people with disabilities, the realities of care arrangements can result in reinforcing passivity and restricting autonomy. This may happen when others take charge of their care, or when carers' views are given priority over the views of those who are cared for.[10] With their interventions, disability-rights movements contribute yet another important angle to the relations of caring required to challenge, rather than entrench, inequality and discrimination.

Ideologies of caring also play a role in the designa-tion of who receives care and who does not within a society. Political activism is often oriented toward challenging the boundaries of care and to whom care is afforded and to whom it is not. In this sense, care can also be part of resistance to dominant ideologies

OUT   39

and existing care structures and institutions, such as
when groups self-organize to engage in mutual aid to
ensure their care, or when people offer help to those
who are neglected and excluded, for example when
supporting refugees.[11]

Ideologies of caring have lately reemerged in a
new guise in the current imperative for self-care.
There is an attempt to fuse self-care with financial
asset management: take care of yourself, because
you are your own most valuable asset, a form of
human capital that will yield high economic returns
if you look after it. But there is also an underside of
insecurity to this imperative: take care of yourself,
because nobody else will, in a context where in many
places public services continue to be squeezed,
collective solidarity is undermined (for example by
stigmatizing welfare), and precarious work becomes
more prevalent.

By unpacking such ideologies of caring, the point
is that we get beyond a simple understanding of care
as an emotional or moral disposition, and drill down
to the structural conditions that impede or facilitate
the availability of and access to sufficient care. In
doing so, it's necessary to think across the spectrum
of paid and unpaid labor, and it's important to turn
previous economic thinking on its head. Instead
of thinking from the requirements of production,
expressed through the economic indicators of productivity, gross domestic product, economic growth,
and so forth, we should start from the perspective of
reproduction, which means all of the activities and
social relationships that make life possible, to which
care belongs.

~~Care: In Crisis~~

Everyone should be able to live a materially secure
and meaningful life premised on emotional well-
being, physical health, fulfilling social relationships,

and an intact ecological environment. Care is in crisis when more and more people are unable to benefit from these basic goods or to get help when access to them is endangered. Care is in crisis when those who provide care to others are unable to do so adequately and under dignified conditions. Care is in crisis when there is a growing gap between care needs and the resources made available to meet them. In an unequal world, no crisis affects everyone equally. It is therefore not simply a case of establishing the existence of a crisis. Instead, the question looms large: a care crisis for whom? There are deep inequalities in the way the crisis is experienced, and in the way that care is organized when this entrenches division and pits us against one another.

In sum, a care crisis refers to the increasing inability of people to access the care they need to live well and the increasingly difficult conditions under which people provide care, both paid and unpaid. Indeed, care-intensive jobs have high occurrences of burnout.[12] So, too, does caring at home due to the constant stress of juggling these demands with those of paid employment.[13] Indeed, burnout, it must be stressed, is "not a problem of people, but of the social environment in which they work."[14] A care crisis refers to the exhaustion of societal care resources in the face of care inequalities. Yet, as we also know with the climate crisis, we cannot keep taking and taking and taking without the chance for resources and capacities to be replenished.

~~Crisis: Dynamics~~

Why is there a care crisis? There is a whole host of factors that are having a combined effect. The relationship between capitalism and care is crisis-prone because the reproduction of the labor force is a prerequisite for capitalist production, but not something systematically provided by profit-oriented businesses. This is why a mitigating role has developed for states to provide social security and public services. Particular historical periods are characterized by specific regimes of care and social reproduction that govern its provision across state, market, and society.[15] In the last years, a crisis of care has been growing, on the one hand because of rising care needs due to demographic changes such as ageing, but also because the societal capacities for care are being systematically run down.

One structural factor is that the "productive deal" between capital and labor in the postwar period of the 20th century has broken down—the reliance of capital on the reproduction of a particular national labor force has been rendered less important due to both globalization and financialization. So too have the accompanying arrangements that went with this: the reproductive role of women who now participate to a far greater extent in the labor force and are therefore not available in the same way as a resource in the home or are overburdened. At the same time, households now on the whole need more than just one income to make ends meet, because overall wages have been stagnating—that is, if people live within a nuclear-family household, also something that is changing. Our lives have become more and more oriented toward our jobs and our employment, not only because we have to, but because ideas of what constitutes meaningful human activity have become intricately bound up with self-actualization and fulfillment through work.[16] At the same time, we have to work to survive. And even if this process has happened to different degrees in different countries, the neoliberal tendency has been for austerity measures to chip away at the welfare state, social security, and public infrastructures, instilling in us the idea that welfare is just something for those who cannot afford to take care of themselves. Increasingly,

care has become of interest to capital, and the logic of
accumulation drives market expansion. Privatization
turns care into a source of private profit making, and
self-care and wellness industries are booming. The
wellness ideology reinforces personal responsibility,
as well as suggesting that you can exercise, supple-
ment, or even mindfully navigate your way out of
every problem—if you can afford to.

And while much of the political debate is couched
in terms of concerns over how to pay for rising
care needs, there is a whole machinery of wealth
extraction operating behind the notion of "cost
efficiency" and "cost saving." For example, in Britain
(which has often served as a laboratory for neoliberal
restructuring) the government's promotion of
privatization, coupled with a regulative environment
permissive to financialization, have exposed the
social care sector to the pursuit of financial profit
with the entry of private-equity firms and outsourc-
ing companies. Private-equity firms usually sell
acquired companies again within three to five years,
with the intention of making a quick profit. Caring is
a time- and labor-intensive activity. Consequently,
efficiency gains in care are mostly "pseudorational-
izations," like reducing the time available for tasks,
redefining what counts as a necessary task and what
does not, or reducing pay and conditions. What is
more, where there is no regulation to prohibit it happening, financial engineering exposes the care sector
to volatility and enables considerable monetary gains
to be made, and tax obligations reduced. In the case
of residential care home chains in Britain, research
has estimated that around ten percent of funds "leak"
out as dividend payments, net interest payments,
directors' fees, and profits before tax.[17]

There are two problems at the heart of the
dynamics described above: First of all, in a capitalist
economy, there is a constant struggle to keep the

cost of care as low as possible lest it eat into profits.
Second, as care is drawn into capitalist markets, the
business models applied impact negatively on the
quality of care and employment conditions, because
care does not lend itself to high profitability and
economies of scale. At the same time, it is subjected
to financialization as a means of nonetheless extract-
ing wealth. Moreover, where windfall profits are
made at one end of the care spectrum, for example
the pharmaceutical industry, they are premised on
the more labor-intensive, low-wage sectors at the
other end of the spectrum, for example health and
social care.[18] When we unpack these structural
dynamics, we see how they are driving inequality.

~~Crisis: Ways Out~~

What, then, are ways out of the care crisis? For a long
time, conventional wisdom has relied on the redis-
tributive potentials of economic growth. The bigger
the proverbial pie, the more there is to go around. Yet,
the doctrine of economic growth rests on a number
of untenable premises. First of all, it has never been
true that economies can keep growing endlessly
and that everyone will thereby be cared for. For one
thing, economic growth does not automatically lead
to its equitable distribution, as the stark increases
in economic inequality and wealth concentration
of the last decades show: between 2011 and 2017,
average wages rose by three percent while dividends
to wealthy shareholders rose by thirty-one percent
in advanced economies.[19] Second, colonialism and
neocolonialism have spurred the exploitation of land,
labor, and resources from countries in the Global
South and severely decreased sustainable livelihoods
for their populations. The planet's ecological limits
urgently demand a different economic model. Third,
the hitherto existing model of economic growth
has relied on keeping the costs of care and social

reproduction as low as possible by drawing on
the unpaid and underpaid work that women have
historically done in the home, and that increasingly
is being off-loaded onto precarious workers in a
devalued care sector. For a long time, this free or
cheap labor went unseen and was simply taken for
granted; but now, as the growth model comes into
crisis and willingness to do low-paid care work
diminishes, the care crisis also becomes more visible,
and the quest for profits eats into the foundation on
which growth was built. The current care crisis, then,
does not demand a return to a better past, but rather
a struggle for a better future.

Everyone needs to be cared for and everyone
needs access to care, although not everyone has the
same needs. Care isn't something that can be a simple
private matter but requires a social infrastructure
to which all have access. Those who need care are
not always the same people as those who are given
it. Nor do those who need care always have the
private resources to pay for it. Care in this sense truly
reveals interdependence. But it is also a profoundly
political question, as debates about the management
of the pandemic remind us. For many years, the
dismantling of welfare states has eroded Western
societies' capacities for providing professional care
and for finding people willing to work in care. All in
all, caring requires a different status and needs to be
organized differently at the level of societal institutions and the practices of the everyday, with regard to
political entitlements as well as ethical commitments
toward one another.

Caring is about relationships in which we both give
and receive care. Nonetheless, it won't be enough to
invoke people's sentiments and call for everyone to
be kinder to one another. Indeed, considering how
ideologies of caring can be instrumentalized, such
calls can even backfire. Capitalism has long depended

on the compassion and sense of responsibility for others that is the staple of the "invisibilized" and undervalued work of care and social reproduction. Particularly in times of crisis, empathy, compassion, and a sense of responsibility are mobilized in order to keep care afloat under adverse conditions.

Neither will it be enough to shower those who care with symbolic appreciation or offer one-off bonus payments to care workers, as happened in the coronavirus pandemic. Truly valuing care means allocating more time, money, and societal capacities to caring across the life course. Professional care workers require secure employment with adequate remuneration and better working conditions. More resources are required to enable hiring more staff, providing the materials and resources required to do the job well, along with training and opportunities for further qualification, time and means for exchange with coworkers, and the recognition of trade unions and collective bargaining. Making employment more attractive is the condition for attracting the many more workers who are needed to meet the care requirements of both the present and future. This also means elevating care's undervalued status and requires an adequately funded public infrastructure, which can be paid for by progressive taxation, sustained increases in corporation tax, and even a wealth tax.

Collective care requires institutions that can organize and allocate the necessary resources. But this shouldn't mean top-down centralized management of care services run by bureaucrats and paternalism. Democracy is not merely the negotia-tion of interests, nor is it simply about participation; it pertains equally to the *scope* and *processes* of, as well as *ability to effect*, decision-making. Democratizing care means involving care givers and receivers in an equal and bottom-up process. There is a wealth of experience and experimentation among grassroots social movements that confront the injustices of existing conditions for care while organizing care for those who need it. Grassroots social movements often create alternative structures through which people can sustain their livelihood without having to find the money to purchase increasingly expensive commodities and commodified services. For a long time, self-help groups—in mental health for instance—have often emerged to provide more effective kinds of care and to be critical of exclusion, marginalization, or professionalized top-down services on their own terms. What do new collective and cooperative ownership models of caring look like in the present context?

Bottom-up organization is not only needed in order to follow principles of democracy. Nobody wants the anonymity of professionalization and the logic of professionalized care to determine all of their social relations. Nor can all of society's care needs be met by professional, paid carers—nobody would seriously want that. Not only would this be inordinately expensive, but caring for ourselves and each other is a crucial part of our social and intimate lives. However, there needs to be a redistribution of care work. This means having time to care against the ways in which waged work engulfs our lives and reclaiming time from waged work, for example through demanding a shorter working week, while also expanding our networks of caring beyond the privatized realms of the nuclear family. Reversing the trend toward privatizing and individualizing the responsibility and the cost of care is not simply a moral imperative; it can also help to devise more effective and efficient forms of care that are more integrated across everyday life. And yet, current struggles for more and better care can be about building a different kind of society, not simply

improving care systems to the extent that capital
accumulation can continue with the relations of
exploitation and inequality on which it is premised.
Instead, reclaiming caring against the logics of
unbounded productivism and economic growth that
dominate our lives can be a valuable starting point
for charting ways out of the care crisis.

48 THE   WA

1 UNI Global Union, *Risking Their Lives to Help Others Survive: A Survey of Nursing Home and In-Home Care Workers in 37 Countries* (Nyon: UNI Global Union, 2021).

2 World Health Organisation, *Preventing and Managing COVID-19 Across Long-Term Care Services: Policy Brief* (Geneva: World Health Organisation, 2020).

3 Berenice Fisher and Joan C. Tronto, "Toward a Feminist Theory of Caring," in *Circles of Care: Work and Identity in Women's Lives*, ed. Emily K. Abel and Margaret K. Nelson (Albany: State University of New York Press, 1990), pp. 36–62.

4 Mariarosa Dalla Costa, "Women and the Subversion of Community," in *The Power of Women and the Subversion of Community*, by Mariarosa Dalla Costa and Selma James (Bristol: Falling Wall Press, 1972), pp. 21–56; Silvia Federici, *Wages Against Housework* (London: Power of Women Collective; Bristol: Falling Wall Press, 1975).

5 International Labour Organization, *Care Work and Care Jobs for the Future of Decent Work* (Geneva: International Labour Office, 2018), pp. 168 and 38–39.

6 For more information on informal care in Austria, see Martin Nagl-Cupal et al., *Angehörigenpflege in Österreich: Einsicht in die Situation pflegender Angehöriger und in die Entwicklung informeller Pflegenetzwerke* (Vienna: Bundesministerium für Arbeit, Soziales, Gesundheit und Konsumentenschutz, 2018).

7 For more information on twenty-four-hour live-in care in Austria, Germany, and Switzerland, see Brigitte Aulenbacher, Helma Lutz, and Karin Schwiter, eds., *Gute Sorge ohne gute Arbeit? Live-in-Care in Deutschland, Österreich und der Schweiz* (Weinheim: Beltz Juventa, 2021).

8 In Austria, median gross hourly earnings in 2018 were slightly above fifteen euros. In Slovakia, the Czech Republic, and Romania, they were well below ten euros, and in Bulgaria even below five euros. See "Earning Statistics," Eurostat, March 1, 2021, https://ec.europa.eu/eurostat/statistics-explained/images/c/c7/Median_gross_hourly_earnings%2C_all_employees_%28excluding_apprentices%29%2C_2018.png, accessed November 27, 2021.

9 Peter Beresford, *What Future for Care? Viewpoint Informing Debate* (York: Joseph Rowntree Foundation, 2008), p. 9.

10 Ibid.

11 Valeria Graziano, Marcell Mars, and Tomislav Medak, "Care and Its Discontents," in *New Alphabet School* (Berlin: Haus der Kulturen der Welt, 2020), https://newalphabetschool.hkw.de/care-and-its-discontents/, accessed November 27, 2021.

12 This was already so prior to the pandemic; see Eurofound, *Burnout in the Workplace: A Review of Data and Policy Responses in the EU* (Luxembourg: Publications Office of the European Union, 2018), p. 7.

13 Eliana Dockterman, "42% of Women Say They Have Consistently Felt Burned Out at Work in 2021," *Time*, September 27, 2021, https://time.com/6101751/burnout-women-in-the-workplace-2021/, accessed November 27, 2021.

14 Christina Maslach, "Understanding Job Burnout," in *Stress and Quality of Working Life: Current Perspectives in Occupational Health*, ed. Ana Maria Rossi, Pamela L. Perrewé, and Steven L. Slauter (Greenwich, CT:

OUT

Information Age Publishing,
2006), pp. 37–52; p. 50.

15 Nancy Fraser, "Contradictions
of Capital and Care," *New Left
Review* 100 (2016): pp. 99–117.

16 Kathi Weeks, *The Problem with
Work: Feminism, Marxism,
Antiwork Politics, and Postwork
Imaginaries* (Durham, NC:
Duke University Press, 2011).

17 Vivek Kotecha, *Plugging the Leaks
in the UK Care Home Industry:
Strategies for Resolving the
Financial Crisis in the Residential
and Nursing Home Sector*
(London: Centre for Health and
the Public Interest, 2019).

18 Gabriel Winant, *The Next Shift:
The Fall of Industry and the
Rise of Health Care in Rust Belt
America* (Cambridge, MA: Harvard
University Press, 2021), p. 2.

19 Max Lawson et al., *Time to
Care: Underpaid and Unpaid
Care Work and the Global
Inequality Crisis* (London: Oxfam
International, 2020), p. 11.

50 THE

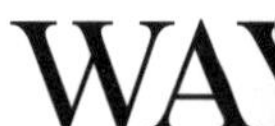

The Way Out of Digital Capitalism

Evgeny Morozov

OUT 53

54 THE   WAY

Let me start by revealing that the initial suggestion,
from the organizers of steirischer herbst, for the title
of my talk was "The Way Out of Digital Feudalism."
I immediately rejected it, thinking that we should
set our task more ambitiously, and, as they used to
say back in the day, name the system—but name it
correctly. I do think that one of the many problems
with the current digital debate is this tendency to
misallocate the blame; that is, quite often we hear
people talking about Big Tech as if it were some kind
of bad apple that came out of nowhere and is not
connected to the rest of capitalism or Wall Street or
the military-industrial complex.

Informed by such simplistic and partial accounts,
it's easy to think that the contemporary situation
is problematic not because of certain structural
problems with capitalism, but simply because we
have too many bad apples (or Apples, I guess) that
have become too big—and we can fix things by just
making them smaller. As if, once we moved from
one Instagram to a hundred Instagrams, we could
magically find a way out of digital capitalism. In
some ways, this vision is even more utopian than the
techno-utopianism that, for the past twenty years,
has come out of Silicon Valley. And I think that we
have to be realistic, and I will try to get us to that
realism.

However, it's very important to start by asking a
simple question: Why is it that, just as we're living
through one of the most profound transformations
of digital infrastructures—think artificial intelligence
and cloud computing—we also seem unable to
imagine a better way of organizing our social,
political, and economic affairs that would not default
to capitalism? This, I'd argue, is not just a matter of
us being unable to find more creative uses for digital
infrastructures. It's, of course, also the consequence
of a profound and existential intellectual crisis on the

left, which no longer knows what it wants. Thus, in a zombie-like fashion, almost algorithmically, the left keeps repeating the slogans that it inherited from the 19th century and from the workers' movement.

It's not necessarily that those slogans are bad or outdated. Nor is it that the struggles of workers are no longer relevant; they are. It's just that one would have thought that in the third decade of the 21st century, the left would be able to imagine a new political project that would truly leverage the power of deploying artificial intelligence, platforms, and data, but do so in a way that wouldn't just be a minor, technical improvement on the system of central planning, which does seem like a prospect that excites so many on the left. It could, of course, be much worse, with many on the left dreaming about finding ways to humanize the current system, which they misdiagnose as surveillance capitalism. Others are trying to build a more cooperative and responsible equivalent of Silicon Valley platforms, but this time owned and run by their users and workers. There's nothing bad about this per se, but, again, it stops short of fully utilizing the radical possibilities that digital technologies seem to offer. Why surrender this field—and the ability to shape and define the social imaginary—to the likes of Elon Musk and Jeff Bezos? As I've mentioned already, I think it has to do with the structural intellectual crisis on the left. Alas, we won't be able to resolve that crisis in this contribution. But I will try at least to hint at what it is and how some of the most difficult conceptual difficulties could be overcome.

Before we get to the prescriptive part, let me say a few words about what I find insufficient or wrong in the current framings of the "digital problem." We can start by examining the account that Shoshana Zuboff gives when she laments the hegemony of "surveillance capitalism."[1] When you look at her theory

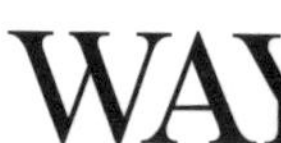

for the first time, it seems to make a lot of sense, at least intuitively. There is surely a lot of surveillance happening all around us. And there is clearly a lot of capitalism happening. So, a term like "surveillance capitalism" seems to make sense. However, as you start digging deeper, you understand that this is a theory that has nothing critical to say about capitalism itself. It kind of approves of capitalism as a great, highly efficient, increasingly progressive—that is, it gets better over time—system for satisfying human needs, even as those needs themselves become more complex and multidimensional. Thus, a theory of surveillance capitalism doesn't really posit the existence of an alternative system of any kind—it's happy with capitalism, we just need to dial down on all that surveillance. So Zuboff fills a lot of pages attacking today's digital economy—with Google and Facebook in the lead—which she presents as a deviation from the true path. And the true path, under an alternative system that Zuboff calls "information capitalism," is the one trodden by Steve Jobs and Apple. Apparently, salvation is to be found in their hyperbranded devices, which promise us—at a heavy premium that their price commands over alternative models—rebellion as a service. We can simply buy our way out of "surveillance capitalism," it seems. The viability of the "surveillance capitalism" framing, as a political program, hinges upon us accepting that humanizing "information capitalism"—with enlightened capitalists like Steve Jobs or Tim Cook at the helm—is the only way forward. The uptake of this framing by some people on the left attests to its inability to make sense of both digital economy and capitalism.

We also see plenty of smart, leftist people out there who are now advocating the importance of democratizing data ownership or treating data as a common good. However, it's not at all obvious how in itself, all those calls for turning data into a common good are going to resolve the fundamental tensions inside capitalism. How is that going to get us away from the immense dependence that our governments have developed on the financial sector? Or how are these measures going to get us away from today's status quo, where those who happen to own assets like houses are clearly in a much better position that those who don't?

These questions, on first sight, seem to lie completely outside of the digital focus, so, one might ask, why even bother talking about them? This is where we have to be very careful about throwing around terms like "digital capitalism." We have to be careful not to present digital capitalism as something that stands apart, completely on the outside, from the capitalism of Wall Street, the Pentagon, and the oil companies. It's not as if there's a separate digital economy that revolves around data, not capital. The "digital" in "digital capitalism" is no mere qualifier; it's a nod to reality. Today, all capitalism is digital: oil companies are digital, banks are digital, everything is digital. This doesn't mean, though, that the solutions to the challenges of digital capitalism have to revolve, primarily, about the question of redistributing rights to the ownership of data or to the use of, and access to, various digital infrastructures. The forward-looking and comprehensive agenda of transformation can include them, but it cannot default to them—and them only.

In a true dialectical fashion, we should also look beyond the left for a second. On the right, we get a somewhat different picture of the digital and its potential. We get a lot of people who essentially celebrate disruption for the same reason why Marx and Engels celebrated capitalism, that is, it melts all that is solid into air—except that Marx and Engels celebrated capitalism for disrupting the institutions of feudalism and tradition, with their undoubtedly reactionary impact on the rest of society. Today's proud neoliberals celebrate the disruption of the various institutions of the welfare and administrative state instead, whether it's the public university or the public hospital or the public library or the public transportation system.

All of them, in one way or another, are finding themselves under assault by the well-funded digital players. Many of them are able to dump so much money into this sector solely because of the particular conjuncture of the global economy: since the interest rates are extremely low, there are relatively few investment opportunities that offer high returns beyond Big Tech. Thus, a lot of money from high-net-worth individuals, sovereign wealth funds, even blue-chip corporations like Daimler, ends up flowing into tech companies—and from them, it flows to disrupt the rest of society.

The underlying idea, however, is very simple: by relying on the competitive pressures built into the capitalist system itself, we will be able to discipline those institutions that survive. Those that don't survive, well, we'll replace some of them with platforms. This will be a major step toward the emergence of a more efficient society, where consumers spend less to buy goods and services and where producers also charge less because there's competition and because they're essentially able to tap into the power of data, networks, and algorithms in order to provide their services in a more cost-efficient way.

This efficiency-driven explanation of the magic behind the digital economy where we pay so little for Uber rides or Airbnb stays deserves closer scrutiny. A lot of what appears as digitally-driven efficiency gains revolves around the myth of Silicon Valley being this magnet of innovation, with young Steve Jobs working sleepless nights in the garages of Palo Alto. But this has little to do with reality, for the real reason that the low cost of some of these services is unrelated to the power of innovation. Rather, it has more to do with the existence, after the financial crisis, of the giant pools of money—think about SoftBank's $100 billion Vision Fund—that absorb the losses of the companies they invest in (like Uber, for example). These funds can easily sustain losses of five, six, ten billion dollars—sometimes stretched over several years—in order to see their chosen platform crush all competition. So, it's normal for these firms to temporarily keep the rates low and sustain losses; if their competitors are not as deep-pocketed as SoftBank, they will probably fold and go under much earlier.

It's a very standard dynamic inside the capitalist system. And it's playing itself perfectly in the current digital capitalist system, right? The difference is that a lot of people inside Silicon Valley are managing to hide under the rhetoric of efficiency, disruption, innovation, et cetera, which is a little bit harder to swallow in 2021 than in, say, 2013, but we swallow it nonetheless.

When a lot of governments welcome the intrusion of these firms into their markets, they're expecting, not unreasonably but quite naively, that these companies will help alleviate the burden that the provision of important services by the state itself is exercising on public budgets. And you're now seeing this repeat itself with the intrusion of Big Tech not just into transportation or financial services or hospitality services, as it was before, but specifically in the context of the postpandemic recovery, with their intrusion into the education and health care systems. The pandemic has opened the doors for Big Tech, already transforming the provision of many public services and sucking in a lot of data.

The narrative of efficiency that the proponents of furthering the neoliberal digitization of society invoke to justify further intrusions appears to be based on myth. What, however, about the insistence that we should make this industry more competitive? Personally, I don't really see what problem is being solved by this, other than maybe the curtailing of the political and lobbying power of Big Tech. That power, of course, is not trivial and we shouldn't minimize possible repercussions. But, as far as the shrinkage of the political imagination on the left is concerned, not much will be solved by making sure that Facebook sells off Instagram and WhatsApp. One can, of course, expect all sorts of miracles from the intensified market competition—but that's more traditionally an expectation from the right, not from the left. As long as we're clear that we expect progress to happen by means of more markets, not fewer, there's no problem: it's a respectable position on the right—and whoever on the left wants to jump on that bandwagon should do it in full awareness of where that train is likely to arrive.

There's one radical position that I haven't yet explored. Before I do that, we can draw an interim conclusion of some kind: none of the mainstream approaches, on both the left and right, actually aspire to transcend capitalism, whatever it is that they say about the transcendence of its digital component. So, what about this other, more radical position that I haven't yet explored? Here I'm talking primarily about the demands of those who are advocating the deployment of AI, Big Data, and digital infrastructures (that is, the Internet of Things or the smart city) in order to reinvent central planning.

Of course, it's a bit of a historical curiosity that now, more than three decades after the fall of the Berlin Wall, we're observing a push to revive central planning. The tools may have changed but the underlying logic hasn't: its proponents insist that it is only by rationalizing the capitalist economy that we would be able to tame some of its most turbulent dynamics. The goal, then, is to simplify and rationalize, to subject to bureaucratic control—this time, by means of permanent digital monitoring and analysis, courtesy of Big Data.

There are, of course, strong and weak versions of this thesis; someone like Paul Cockshott, a seasoned participant in the so-called socialist calculation debate, is in the former camp.[2] A lot of mainstream and trendy projects—like fully automated luxury communism[3]—tend to endorse, in one way or another, the weaker version. What's common to both versions, however, is the idea that we should start by simplifying and rationalizing what Marx used to call the "realm of necessity." And it's only by fully rationalizing and optimizing what's happening in that realm, that is, by making sure that we're all well-fed, that we have warm clothes and a place to sleep, that we'll be able to arrive at the communist utopia and finally shift our focus to sorting out the "realm of freedom."

There are many arguments within Marxist theory as to whether the realm of freedom can also be established in the realm of necessity, that is, to what extent work can become play and lose its alienating dimension. These are fascinating discussions, but, by and large, today they represent the margins of the debate. The more modest task, as many of today's technologically literate leftists see it, is to make sure that everything is running smoothly, with automation and artificial intelligence taking care of all the mundane processes, so that people can finally be left to themselves and choose what they want to do, whether it will be writing poetry or drinking wine or fishing.

Conceived this way, the realm of freedom is something that does not require much organization or planning. So, the hope goes, we'll use digital technologies to make sure that the basic needs are mapped and met in the most rational, fastest, and easiest way possible, if needed through planning and automation. And whatever happens next will be the true apotheosis of freedom and creativity. But we don't really need to be concerned about it; as long as decisions in that realm are taken democratically, there's not much else to worry about.

A lot of conceptual blockages on the left derive from our inability to think differently about this dichotomy of necessity and freedom. One group of people who have tried, and, to some extent, succeeded in operationalizing both realms in their political agenda are, surprisingly, the neoliberals, above all Friedrich Hayek. It's very important to understand that for somebody like Hayek, the market isn't just an instrument for satisfying our needs in the realm of necessity. It's not just the method of allocating goods. It's not just a method of essentially distributing houses or cars or shoes in the most efficient manner, which is what central planning is supposed to do in the socialist conception. For people like Hayek, the market is also an instrument and an infrastructure of freedom. It's an instrument of discovery of the new, whether new techniques of production or new tastes. For like-minded thinkers, like James M. Buchanan, the market is also an infrastructure of becoming where we try different identities and ways of being; it's in the market that we become free. We can, of course, question the completion or the depth of the emancipatory visions in the broader neoliberal project; much of the supposed liberation here revolves around consumption and specifically around ideas of consumer sovereignty. So, one might say that this is not a very sophisticated idea of freedom. But what the neoliberals do deliver— and quite effectively, if I may say so—is the merging

of the two realms into a single infrastructure, and that
infrastructure is the market.

If you reread the last seventy years of the socialist
calculation debate—starting with Ludwig von Mises
and ending with Buchanan—you'll see the broader
intellectual shift in the arguments advanced by
neoliberals, from markets as superior calculating
devices for allocation to markets as infrastructures
of progress, becoming, and discovery. Nothing of
the kind happens in traditional socialism, where the
arguments have, throughout the last one hundred
years, been mostly about allocation. The socialists
could never operationalize central planning as an
infrastructure of both satisfying our needs and
necessities and catering to creativity, becoming,
discovery, and freedom. That's just not what central
planning is supposed to do. Moreover, it's not
supposed to do it in the way that markets do. For
somebody like Hayek, it's clear that as societies
become more complex, new ways of social coordination are needed—but they're needed not to simplify
social interactions but to enable more complex forms
of them. Central planning, when it works as intended,
seems to do the opposite: it wants to simplify and
rationalize the realm of necessity, so that we can
become more creative and maybe even complex in
the realm of freedom.

The reality is that the plan—the simple infrastructure that undergirds that traditional vision
for socialism—is geared toward just one thing: the
resolution of our basic needs in the simplest manner
possible. Everything else is supposed to happen on
the outside without infrastructure, and in a kind of
haphazard manner. And it's the very randomness of
that process that often gets celebrated by socialists,
with many of them adopting the liberal hat and
proclaiming that we should just leave people to
their own devices. Thus, as long as we organize their

production, consumption, food intake, sleeping habits, and whatever, we don't actually need to worry about how they spend the rest of their time. And it's precisely the fact that we don't worry about this last bit that ensures that we remain free. And I'm just not sure that this is the correct position for socialists to take. It's a wrong-headed position, and, no matter how many digital accoutrements you put on top, its wrong-headedness will still be there.

Let me say just a few words about what an alternative vision would be like. Instead of dividing our time between work and play, with technology allowing us to vastly improve the former, we should assume that all action has a creative potential in it. That potential is not always activated, but by manipulating the circumstances in which we act, we can at least maximize the chances that it would. The right social institutions and digital infrastructures could, in fact, facilitate that. That creative potential is precisely what would allow us to generate the kind of wealth that, in the capitalist language, goes under the label of "innovation." Right now, it takes an army of start-ups and entrepreneurs to do it—but this is precisely because our social institutions and digital technologies have been configured in such a way as to deprive all the other actors from playing an active role in this process.

Instead of building a socialist society which further entrenches the division between work and play, necessity and freedom, we should be building a system where value is produced as we go about living our lives, whether it involves repairing broken washing machines or learning languages or writing essays. Many of these activities right now happen in a very isolated, analog manner; whatever creative solutions we invent when working on them die a quiet death in our own heads—they're never shared with others, unless, of course, we're motivated by the pursuit of wealth and can turn some creative idea for fixing a washing machine into an app. Today, capitalism is the only system capable of taking these tiny innovations and scaling them up to the level of the system.

Socialism, as it's conditionally conceived, is not even contemplating doing something similar, hoping that governments would find much better solutions in a rational, centralized manner. But that's beside the point: there's no reason why socialism shouldn't take advantage of the immense creativity of its subjects—and not just in the workplace but in everyday life. To do that, we do need new institutions and new infrastructures. Yes, we might not yet have a total vision of how everything would work, but one thing is clear: unless we work to preserve some maneuvering space, both with regards to the mere possibility of having powerful nonmarket institutions and digital infrastructures that are not under control of Big Tech or the smaller crypto overlords, that project wouldn't be possible at all. The time to act is now.

WA

1   Shoshana Zuboff, *The Age of
    Surveillance Capitalism: The
    Fight for a Human Future at
    the New Frontier of Power*
    (London: Profile, 2019).
2   W. Paul Cockshott and Allin F.
    Cottrell, *Towards a New Socialism*
    (Spokesman: Nottingham, 1993).
3   Aaron Bastani, *Fully Automated
    Luxury Communism: A Manifesto*
    (London: Verso, 2019).

OUT

68 THE WAY

The Way Out of Globalism: Polanyi, Schmitt, and the Market Golem

Quinn Slobodian

70 THE WAY

The opposition between the global and the national has become so reflexive in recent decades that it can be hard to remember that there are other alternatives. Yet two thinkers in the middle of the 20th century from very different political backgrounds found their way to an alternative political geography that was neither global nor national. Although much has been written about these thinkers, they have rarely if ever been put into conversation. They are Karl Polanyi and Carl Schmitt. Part of the reason why the two thinkers are seldom paired is because their politics seem so incompatible. Polanyi, born in Vienna in 1886, has been seen as a critic of neoliberalism avant la lettre, a liberal in his early years followed by a turn toward social democracy in his later decades. Schmitt, born two years after Polanyi in a small town in western Germany, was a card-carrying member of the Nazi Party from 1933, and remained a conservative until the end of his long life in 1985.

In the text that follows, I find my way to their surprisingly parallel proposals for a way out of globalism and their common rejection of what Polanyi called "universal capitalism."[1] I do so mostly through an investigation of their use of metaphors—specifically the metaphors of the man-machine, the Leviathan, and the golem. As we shall see, it is in their reflection on the interface between the human and technology that the seed of their alternative political geography can be found.

Let's begin with Polanyi's most famous metaphor, one so successful that it has seeped into common sense and shaken off common knowledge of its authorship. This is the idea of the "self-regulating market," a metaphor that Polanyi began using in the 1940s, possibly inspired by the work of his brother, Michael Polanyi, a chemist and early neoliberal who favored analogies between capitalist societies and homeostatic systems premised on tacit knowledge. Karl Polanyi's deployment of the metaphor of the "self-regulating market" is subtle. He performs a three-step that goes something like this: First, the discipline of economics presupposes a self-regulating market that seeks equilibrium and a perfect correspondence between supply and demand mediated by the price mechanism. He acknowledges this is a fiction—a conjecture within a specific epistemological field—the field of neoclassical economics. Polanyi's second step is the *unmasking* of this fiction. He observed famously that "laissez-faire was planned," institutions are always necessary for capitalism, markets are always "embedded," self-regulating markets *could only* be a fantasy or else humanity would be ground to dust, that the iron fist of violent conquest accompanies the creation of new markets, et cetera.[2] Much of the important research done in the field of economic sociology and the global history of capitalism works in the register of this second point: the unmasking of the fiction of the self-regulating market. But Polanyi has a third step waiting. The third step is that the fantasy has real effects. As Gareth Dale quotes Polanyi in his intellectual biography: "It is a spectral world in which the specters are real."[3] The very attempt to realize the fantastical conjecture ends up transforming all of our lives.[4]

But there is something unsatisfying about the way that conversations around the self-regulating market go. They tend to a kind of circularity and, as some critics have pointed out, tend to reify the very division that Polanyi is seeking to undo.[5] What happens if we rummage around in Polanyi for different metaphors?

One that jumps out is that of *the golem* and the related metaphors of the giant, the automaton, and the man-machine. There is a wonderful line from

Polanyi in a letter from 1960 that captures much of
what this metaphor did for him, and what I will elab-
orate on for the remainder of this text: "The blessing
and curse of the machine is what set us on this road.
Our destiny was to become a society that, thanks to
the power of machines, has grown into a giant, but
one that renders the individual powerless."[6]

Putting Polanyi alongside Schmitt, we find
something interesting. They both use the metaphor
of the golem, but they use it in different ways. Schmitt
thought about the problem of the golem in relation to
the state. In his 1938 book on Hobbes's *Leviathan*, he
says three different times that it is often feared that
the Leviathan of the state will grow into a "Moloch
or a Golem" or "an all-demanding Moloch or an
all-trampling Golem," as he puts it at one point.[7]
Polanyi, by contrast, thought about the golem in
relation to the market and the economy.

The state and the economy are the two spheres
that Schmitt and Polanyi saw the 19th century as
invested in both creating and then separating from
one another. They are otherwise known by the
Kantian and Roman categories that Schmitt uses
in *The Nomos of the Earth*: those of *dominium* (the
sphere of property and ownership) and *imperium* (the
space of government and sovereignty).[8] Comparing
Polanyi and Schmitt, we find that they use the
metaphor of the golem differently, and yet their
political geography curiously enough ends up in a
very similar place by the end of World War II. They
both fear the universalism of the United States as
the bearer of this golem-like spirit. Both worry that
the United States is the man–machine incarnate and
that its global conception of its own mandate in the
world is something that needs to be militated against
and prevented from realization. They both became
proponents of what we could call a pluriverse.[9]
Polanyi called his proposal *Tame Empires* in the

title of the book that he proposed to follow up *The Great Transformation*, and Schmitt called them great spaces (Großräume).[10] Polanyi ended World War II writing an article called "Universal Capitalism or Regional Planning?"; Schmitt wrote an article pitting "Great Spaces against Universalism."[11]

How did they get there? Dwelling on the metaphor of the golem helps us draw connections between periods of Polanyi's life that are often kept separate from one another. His experience in Budapest helping launch a radical bourgeois party after World War I is often seen as a distinct era from his later turn to democratic socialism in Vienna, London, the United States, and Canada. But the division may not be altogether tenable. Let's think about the metaphor of the golem to ask why.

The metaphor of the golem, which was primarily a Jewish folk tale in the 19th century, entered the limelight during World War I. The scholar Maya Barzilai credits its popularity to the novel titled, simply, *The Golem*, by Gustav Meyrink, which sold close to 200,000 copies—she calls it "the *Da Vinci Code* of its day"—and the series of successful films made in German studios on the same theme. Common to the written and visual texts, she writes, is the motif of "the strong protector turning into a violent destroyer."[12] The common meaning of the golem metaphor at the time was a technologically enabled juggernaut of which thinking humans had lost control. After World War I, Polanyi wrote to a cousin that "humanity is a golem which stares with horror at its own frozen mask, a tortured soul at the terrible machine."[13] Over the years, Polanyi would use a similar metaphor to describe the market in just this way. Perhaps most famous is his reference to a "gargantuan automaton" in the passage in *The Great Transformation* when he writes that "world trade now meant in the 19th century the organizing of life on the planet under a self-regulating market, comprising labor, land, and money, with the gold standard as the guardian of this gargantuan automaton. Nations and peoples were mere puppets in the show utterly beyond their control."[14] We can see in a passage like this how Polanyi skips happily between the three different registers I described at the beginning. This is a conjecture, but also a real conjecture, and one that, despite its fantastic essence, is producing a real-life cataclysm (to use another of his favored terms). Polanyi's writing is at its most powerful when it shows in vivid detail the dirty business in the movement between these last two registers: in the drive to make the fantasy real.

It is also here that Polanyi gives us another handhold for his use of metaphor. In his description of colonialism in *The Great Transformation*, he writes that "the natives are forced to make a living by selling their labor … thus the colonist may decide to cut the breadfruit trees down in order to create an artificial food scarcity or may impose a tax on the native to force him to barter away his labor." He saw a continuity with a preceding early modern era of capitalism in Europe itself: "What the white man may still occasionally practice in remote regions today, namely the smashing up of social structures in order to extract the element of labor from them, was done in the 18th century to white populations by white men for similar purposes."[15] In colonialism and enclosure, Polanyi saw a process of disassembly and reassembly, a kind of techno-surgery. As he put it: "To detach man from the soil meant the dissolution of the body economic into its elements so that each element could fit into that part of the system where it was most useful."[16] This was literally the production of a kind of patchwork humanoid.

Polanyi differentiated between the Hobbesian Leviathan about which Schmitt wrote and his own

vision. "Hobbes's grotesque vision of the state,"
he wrote, "a human Leviathan whose vast body
was made up of an infinite number of human
bodies—was dwarfed by the Ricardian construct of
the labor market: a flow of human lives the supply
of which was regulated by the amount of food put at
their disposal."[17] The Ricardian golem dwarfed the
Hobbesian Leviathan because the state is only one
segment of the world's territory, while the Ricardian
golem swallows the entirety. It is composed of human
components from all of the world's habitable surface.
The question of scale is essential because it draws
attention to the question of how one controls the
golem. In fact, we can understand Polanyi's entire
political project as a problem of taming the golem. I
use *taming* advisedly. His desire is not to kill or slay. If
you think of the golem or the self-regulating automaton as the domain of "the economy" as conceived in
a narrowly neoclassical sense, then even this is not
something that Polanyi wants to see vanish from the
earth. One of the ways in which Polanyi is misrecog-
nized is by people who want to understand political
economic imaginaries in terms of overly stark
binaries: either the commodification of everything *or*
the decommodification of everything. In fact, Polanyi
wanted the commodification of *some* things but,
famously, not all of them: not land, labor, and money.

The golem of the commodity logic and its
grotesque hypertrophy was the object of a vexed
lifelong engagement for Polanyi. How big was too
big? What were the limits of the market? What could
be absorbed into the monstrous assemblage of the
market golem's body and what could not? What
must not? How could the automaton be prevented
from slipping the bonds of its human masters?

He ended up with two basic solutions. The first
was to give the golem a mind. The bracingly counterintuitive quality of Polanyi's writing right after

World War I lies in how strongly he was opposing the lionization of the working class. Why was he skeptical of the wisdom of the workers? Most importantly, they had marched happily into war. Socialist internationalism had proved to be a paper tiger. Polanyi came to the conclusion in the wake of the Great War that it must be the *intellectual* workers and not the manual workers who were the key political class. For one thing, their work was more taxing. "Physical work," he wrote in 1919, "turns the human body into a machine, and such work ought not to be idealised, but abolished."[18] Intellectual labor, by contrast, was "the most exhausting, most excruciating and most productive labour." In the end, intellectual labor was also more important than manual labor: it was "the organizer and director of all other kinds of labour, the originator and guarantor of the productivity of all other forms of labour." It was "entrepreneurs, industrialists and merchants" who came up with new ways to mobilize human resources, to organize collective action, to engineer social outcomes.[19] These were the true Promethean figures in the body politic, and it was they whom Polanyi believed needed to be courted for any successful political project.

In this sense, and at this time, Polanyi had a lot in common with someone like Friedrich Hayek, who also believed that a privileged class of intellectually adept thinkers had a special role to play in producing a productive and stable future. Hayek and Polanyi also had a shared belief in the need to persuade people who did not think of themselves as intellectuals that they were, in fact, intellectuals. What Polanyi was staging in his concentration on winning over the business leader, the shopkeeper, the investor to the idea they were part of the intellectual working class was the defense of an elite-led political mobilization. Why did he put his faith in the grand and petit bourgeoisie rather than the proletariat? Because he believed that the working class was fated to become appendages of the golem: "Physical work turns the body into a machine." They had neither the capacity nor the means to resist their own incorporation into the automaton. The self-regulating market as market golem was pure private ordering by an entrepreneurial and financial class that failed to recognize its own status as a governing class in nuce. They were an acephalic bourgeoisie, filled with disavowed intellectual workers. Given this absence of a head, when endowed with the power of the machine, they form an unreflective bloc with the workers themselves to run amok. This was the failure of the hand to recognize its need for the head.

Seeing this aspect of Polanyi as a prophet of radical intellectual workerism helps explain his ongoing popularity in some circles. Someone like Thomas Piketty is a perfect heir to the early Polanyi in his belief that the golem could be tamed by giving it a brain. The message is: persuade the elites, persuade the policy-making class, produce better technocrats, do what you can to foment a new consensus about how the golem can be slowed in its omnivorous path and can be brought to work for people instead of people working for it, escaping a world where prices "rule everything but nobody ruled them," as Polanyi put it in 1922.[20]

If one of the solutions was to give the golem a brain—by which we can say he means to convert parts of the business elite and conscript them into the project of stabilizing a market-based system—then his other proposal was to render the golem in pieces. This more radical plan emerged from his rapidly changing ideas of political geography. At the beginning of the war, Polanyi was still a staunch globalist. He adhered to the belief, common at the time and since, that global problems needed global solutions, that the League of Nations was a failure because of its lack of support from the leading powers, not because of its attempt to take on a universal role, and that the nation-state was an obsolete container for politics in an interdependent world.

To offer a supporting quote: Polanyi wrote in 1935 that "the actual forms of material existence of man are those of worldwide interdependence. The political forms of human existence must also be worldwide. Either within the boundaries of a world empire or in those of a world Federation, either through conquest and subjection or by international cooperation—the nations of the globe must be brought within the folds of one embracing body if our civilization is to survive."[21]

Fascinatingly, though, by the end of World War II, Polanyi had begun to propose something very different. And what he proposed in his 1945 article "Universal Capitalism or Regional Planning?" is interesting not only for itself but also because it has provided inspiration to others more recently. When the Harvard economist Dani Rodrik gave a keynote to the International Karl Polanyi Society in 2019, he began by drawing attention to this very text.[22] The sociologist Wolfgang Streeck also pointed to it as an inspiration for future political geographies.[23]

What does the text say? It proposes that the golem must be dismembered for humanity to live. The global market must be cleaved into chunks. In this text and his proposal for what he calls "tame empires" from the mid-1940s, Polanyi talks more than once of "autarch" or "autarkic" empires. He proposed a world divided into a series of regions he describes as "the USA, Latin America, the British Commonwealth, German central Europe, Smuts's colonial zones, India, China and other regions." "The tame empire," he wrote, "need not be any more a utopia."[24] His use of the term *utopia* should not be taken lightly. The original title of his magnum opus,

The Great Transformation, was *The Liberal Utopia*, and he saw the self-regulating market itself (which we can also see as the global market golem) as a utopia in the negative sense. But in the autarkic region—the tame empire—Polanyi found a utopia he was willing to defend; one that could be brought down to earth.

Here is where the remarkable meeting with Schmitt happened. By the time of World War II, they disagreed on the specifics but ended on a similar outcome. Schmitt thought that the Soviet Union was a universalist power seeking world communism, while National Socialism was *not* a universalist ideology but only sought control of the "great space" (Großraum) of Central Europe.[25] Polanyi thought the exact opposite. He believed that National Socialism *was* a universalist project based on a vision of "racial domination." Conversely, he thought that after the expulsion of Leon Trotsky and his version of world revolution, the Soviet Union of the 1940s was no longer universalist in its aspirations. The Soviet Union was better seen as a regional power with claims over its near abroad of Eastern Europe but no mandate to expand beyond that.[26]

So, Schmitt and Polanyi seemed to be at perfect odds. And this would have been true except for their opinion of the United States. Schmitt saw the liberalism of Woodrow Wilson and its universalism as denying politics, as casting the enemy not just as an adversary but as someone beyond and outside of the human community as such.[27] His support for National Socialism was justified formally as the need for a bulwark against the version of what he saw as the world-swallowing end of human meaning and human difference. Polanyi, for his part, although he was a devout globalist into the 1930s, saw the United States by 1945 as the descendant of the 19th century, the standard-bearer of what had formerly been the British-centered world economy. By the mid-20th century, Polanyi saw the United States as the stronghold of the market golem.

As he put it in 1945, "the British Commonwealth and the U.S.S.R. form part of a new system of regional powers, while the United States insists on a universalist conception of world affairs which tallies with her antiquated liberal economy. . . . Americans still believe in a way of life no longer supported by the common people in the rest of the world but which nevertheless implies a universality which commits those who believe in it to re-conquer the globe on its behalf." Under American leadership, he said, "at the heart of world politics there is a universalistic conspiracy to make the world safe for the gold standard."[28]

By 1945, both thinkers saw the United States as the prime enemy, the privileged agent of what Schmitt called "planetary imperialism."[29] And they both had the same solution: don't let the Americans take over the world. Both believed in the need for a pluriverse going beyond what Polanyi called the "racial jigsaw puzzle" of Wilsonian self-determination toward large regional economic groupings.[30] There were clearly other differences. Schmitt's great spaces would operate like Hitler's Europe, the Greater East Asia Co-Prosperity Sphere or the Western Hemisphere of the Monroe Doctrine, with hegemons exerting downward control over lesser powers within their sphere of influence. Polanyi envisioned more horizontality in his regional groupings—an idealized version of the rebuilt Habsburg Empire. Yet both were skeptical of the implications of American universalism, which moved golem-like toward global conquest even against its better judgment.

Thinking about Polanyi and Schmitt's ways out of globalism from the present, after the global financial crisis, after the outbreak of the still-raging global pandemic, it's interesting that no matter what kind of

OUT81

radical demands are being made, few, if any, propose
autarky or self-sufficiency of the kind that Schmitt
and Polanyi were entertaining. Autarky remains
a no-go zone for political imagination in the 21st
century, despite all the talk of decoupling, delinking,
deglobalization, and economic nationalism. More
often than not, we operate in a framework of alternative globalisms rather than genuine efforts to opt out
of global interconnection.

To further illuminate the present, it's worth
returning to some of Schmitt's other oppositions.
As he wrote in the 1940s before the war ended and
again after it had, the binary of land and sea power
no longer held.[31] Land and sea had been joined by
the new space of the air and the new phenomenon
of air power, especially important in the era of the
nuclear bomb. It is easy to misconstrue today's global
geo-economic confrontation as a reprisal of land
against sea: a terrestrial Sinocentric megaregional
order facing an oceanic Atlanticist megaregional
order. China plays up the impression itself through
repeated use of "the silk road" in its Belt and Road
Initiative (BRI) messaging and its description of
cargo trains as "steel camel fleets" poised to replace
container ships trapped in the bottlenecks of 19th-
century waterways.[32] But the BRI is also seaborne
and includes a series of deep-water harbors and
ports, and, more importantly, it is digital—bound up
with social media, payment systems, and manifold
forms of tracking and surveillance.[33] This form of
power is about creating space bound by infrastructure, but it is also about capturing movements and
actions as they range through three dimensions.

Here it is worth turning to another invocation of
the golem—by Norbert Wiener, the father of cybernetics. In his 1964 book *God and Golem Inc.*, what
made the golem distinctive was not that it was just
more powerful than us or had some preprogrammed

directives toward accumulation or destruction. It was not just quantitatively different—an exaggeration of certain human drives. It was qualitatively different too. It was a computer. Specifically, it *saw* differently from us. Wiener distinguished between the pictorial image and the operative image. Operative images "perform the functions of their original, may or may not bear a pictorial likeness to original."[34] Harun Farocki would later call these "operational images," machines creating images for use by other machines: the use of satellite technology to produce knowledge about territories that wasn't strictly representational, the use of heat maps and data points on the human face to see patterns in behavior inscrutable to the naked eye.[35]

The attraction of Polanyi's golem is its absolute inversion of the Hayekian vision of a sublime and unknowable economy-as-catallaxy.[36] Polanyi's golem not only made the market visible. It made the market monstrous, a quasi-human assemblage of economic epistemology, private ordering, and unreflective labor power. But this is also, in Wiener's terms, a pictorial image, an image that looks the way humans see. What is challenging about Wiener's idea of the operative image is that it asks us to see how the golem sees, which, as he says, "may or may not bear a pictorial likeness to the original."

I will conclude with a number of questions: What would it look like to travel with Polanyi and Schmitt out of the industrial age and into the digital one— when the man-machine is not made of stovepipes, turbines, and coal hoppers like the Iron Giant or the Tin Woodsman, but coaxial cables, motherboards, and sensors? If land and sea are obsolete binaries, no longer tenable in the 21st century, perhaps the opposing spheres of economy and state are too? How can we dance out of the line of the three-step that Polanyi has taught us and come up with new

OUT   83

metaphors tailored to the problematic of our
time? What ways out of globalism can we find that
don't rely on the fiction of regional autarky or the
comic-book villain of a man-machine made of steel?
How can we disagree with both Polanyi and Schmitt
without falling into the embrace of American universal capitalism?

1   Karl Polanyi, "Universal Capitalism or Regional Planning?," *The London Quarterly of World Affairs* 10, no. 3 (1945): pp. 86–91.

2   Karl Polanyi, *The Great Transformation* (Boston: Beacon, 2001), p. 147.

3   Gareth Dale, *Karl Polanyi: A Life on the Left* (New York: Columbia University Press, 2016), p. 138.

4   For this interpretation of Polanyi as a forerunner of the economic sociology of performativity, see Fred Block and Margaret R. Somers, *The Power of Market Fundamentalism: Karl Polanyi's Critique* (Cambridge, MA: Harvard University Press, 2014).

5   For this critique, see Melinda Cooper and Martijn Konings, "Contingency and Foundation: Rethinking Money, Debt, and Finance after the Crisis," *The South Atlantic Quarterly* 114, no. 2 (2015): pp. 239–50, here p. 241.

6   Karl Polanyi, "Letter to György Heltai, 21 May 1960," in *The Hungarian Writings*, ed. Gareth Dale (Manchester: Manchester University Press, 2016), p. 232.

7   Carl Schmitt, *The Leviathan in the State Theory of Thomas Hobbes: Meaning and Failure of a Political Symbol* (Westport, CT: Greenwood, 1996), p. 59.

8   Carl Schmitt, *The Nomos of the Earth in the International Law of the Jus Publicum Europaeum* (New York: Telos, 2003), p. 45.

9   On Schmitt and the pluriverse, see Roland Axtmann, "Humanity or Enmity? Carl Schmitt on International Politics," *International Politics* 44 (2007): pp. 531–51, p. 537.

10 Karl Polanyi, "Book Outline and Introduction—'Tame Empires' (1938–9)," Karl Polanyi Archive, Concordia University, http://kpolanyi.scoolaid.net:8080/xmlui/handle/10694/718?show=full, accessed December 20, 2021.

11 Carl Schmitt, "Beschleuniger wider Willen oder: Problematik der westlichen Hemisphäre" (1942), in *Staat, Großraum, Nomos: Arbeiten aus den Jahren 1919-1969*, ed. Günter Maschke (Berlin: Duncker & Humblot, 1995), p. 432.

12 Maya Barzilai, *Golem: Modern Wars and Their Monsters* (New York: New York University Press, 2016), pp. 3–4, 10.

13 Quoted in Dale, *Karl Polanyi* (see note 3), p. 59.

14 Polanyi, *The Great Transformation* (see note 2), p. 226.

15 Ibid., p. 172.

16 Ibid., p. 188.

17 Ibid., p. 172.

18 Karl Polanyi, "Manual and Intellectual Labour" (1919), in *The Hungarian Writings* (see note 6), p. 199.

19 Karl Polanyi, "The Programme and Goals of Radicalism: An Address to the General Assembly of the Radical Party" (1918), in *The Hungarian Writings* (see note 6), pp. 186–7.

20 Quoted in Dale, *Karl Polanyi* (see note 3), p. 83.

21 Karl Polanyi, "The Roots of Pacifism" (1935–6), in *For a New West: Essays, 1919–1958*, ed. Giorgio Resta and Mariavittoria Catanzariti (Cambridge, UK: Polity, 2014), p. 87.

22 Dani Rodrik, "Karl Polanyi and Globalization's Wrong Turn," International Karl Polanyi Conference 2019, ORF RadioKulturhaus, Vienna, May 3, 2019.

23 Wolfgang Streeck, "The International State System after Neoliberalism: Europe between National Democracy and Supranational Centralization," *Crisis and Critique* 7, no. 1 (2020): pp. 214–34, here p. 214.

OUT

24 Polanyi, "Book Outline and
Introduction" (see note 10).

25 Carl Schmitt, "Die letzte globale
Linie" (1943), in *Staat, Großraum,
Nomos* (see note 11), p. 448. See
Joshua Derman, "Carl Schmitt
on Land and Sea," *History of
European Ideas* 37, no. 2 (2011):
pp. 181–89, here p. 182. His use
of the term "great space" built
on a widespread discussion of
this category at the time. See
Joshua Derman, "Prophet of a
Partitioned World: Ferdinand
Fried, 'Great Spaces,' and the
Dialectics of Deglobalization,
1929–1950," *Modern Intellectual
History* 18, no. 3 (2021): pp. 757–81.

26 Polanyi, "Universal Capitalism
or Regional Planning?"
(see note 1), p. 86.

27 Carl Schmitt, *The Concept of the
Political* (Chicago: University of
Chicago Press, 1996), pp. 51–79.

28 Polanyi, "Universal Capitalism
or Regional Planning?"
(see note 1), pp. 87, 91.

29 Schmitt, "Die letzte globale
Linie" (see note 25), p. 448.

30 Polanyi, "Universal Capitalism
or Regional Planning?"
(see note 1), p. 89.

31 Carl Schmitt, "Das Meer gegen das
Land" (1941), in *Staat, Großraum,
Nomos* (see note 11), p. 399.

32 "China Ready to Join Kazakhstan
for Stronger Cooperation in All
Areas: FM," Xinhua, January 22,
2021, http://www.xinhuanet.com/
english/2021-01/22/c_139687951.
htm, accessed December 20, 2021.

33 See Jonathan E. Hillman,
*The Emperor's New Road:
China and the Project of the
Century* (New Haven: Yale
University Press, 2020).

34 Norbert Wiener, *God and Golem,
Inc.: A Comment on Certain
Points where Cybernetics
Impinges on Religion* (Cambridge,
MA: MIT Press, 1964), p. 31.

35 See Harun Farocki, *Eye/Machine
I–III* (2001–3), two-channel
video installations re-edited
to single-channel video (color,
sound), 63 min., Museum of
Modern Art, New York.

36 See Jessica Whyte, "The Invisible
Hand of Friedrich Hayek:
Submission and Spontaneous
Order," *Political Theory* 47,
no. 2 (2019): pp. 156–84.

OUT   87

The Way Out of Uncritical Race Theory?

Mark Terkessidis

In 2021, the Netzwerk Neue Deutsche Medienmacher*innen (Network of New German Media-
Makers) bestowed the parody award Goldene
Kartoffel (Golden Potato) on the entire German
media industry—specifically, in recognition of its
"dismal" debate over so-called identity politics. This
subject, the network wrote, had only been addressed
from the sensational perspective of whether it was
polarizing society—which, given the terrorist attacks
by right-wing factions in Halle and Hanau, the
politically motivated murder of conservative local
politician Walter Lübcke by neo-Nazi extremists in
Hesse, and the entry of right-wing extremists into
every German parliament, seemed extremely dis-
concerting. In this way, said the network, the media
missed a great opportunity to open a discussion on
the subject of "how we can become a just and progressive society that is sensitive to discrimination.
For example, long-form reports or cover stories
could have been used to explain and discuss such
concepts as critical race theory, affirmative action,
and gender-appropriate speech."[1]

There is nothing wrong with the Neue Medienmacher*innen's analysis, and the call for discussion
also seems logical. In the process, it could be worthwhile to look at critical race theory and affirmative
action; however, with regard to the situation in
Germany, the suggestion of only discussing concepts
that originated in the US seems equally discon-
certing. And if we want to hold the conversation in
German, would it be appropriate to call for a *kritische
Rassentheorie* (critical race theory) in order to
increase sensitivity to discrimination, given the fact
that the term *Rassentheorie* (race theory) is always
accompanied by echoes of the Nazi era?

Critical race theory is a term used in the US for a
series of positions that originate primarily in the legal
sector. Following the US civil rights movement, the

idea was to promote legislation that no longer treated racism as an individual, motive-driven international act, but as an organizing principle of society that was embedded in the law (legally anchored "racial" segregation had, in fact, existed in the US prior to that time). Furthermore, critical race theory provided a basis through which experiences of racism could be "testified to" and dealt with in court, and fostered an awareness of how, in certain constellations, attention to different forms of discrimination might be neglected in favor of other forms (that is, intersectionality).

There is no doubt that it can also be worthwhile to apply the insights of critical race theory to other contexts. However, these insights would need to be modified to fit the setting in question, since approaches that predominately apply to Black experiences, and which evolved in connection with a specific local slaveholding society and subsequent "racial" segregation, can scarcely be transposed onto Germany or Austria.

Of course, for some time now in the US, critical race theory has no longer been applied solely to Black experiences, but also to the experiences of people of other backgrounds or ethnic identities who are commonly addressed as people of color (POC; in some cases, this term is further specified as BIPOC in order to include Black or indigenous people). There is no German translation for this term—*Farbige* (colored) would once again be a racist epithet. In a 2009 essay, Kien Nghi Ha wrote that POC refers to "all racialized people of African, Asian, Latin American, Arabic, Jewish, indigenous, or Pacific origins or backgrounds in different proportions. It incorporates all those people who are marginalized by the dominant white culture and collectively demeaned by the violence of colonial traditions and presences."[2]

However, this definition presents several problems. On the one hand, as a person with Latin American origins, Augusto Pinochet could also be classified in retrospect as a POC; on the other, under this definition, all individuals of European descent would count as "white." Again and again, it has been pointed out that terms such as POC are social constructs, and, according to Noah Sow, they even originated purely on the basis of self-perception: "It's quite simple: in this book, I identify all Black people who accept the political term *Black* as Black, and all POCs who accept this term as POCs."[3] The only group to whom this classification does not apply, Sow continues, are "white Germans" (weiße Deutsche): in the discourse of anti-racism, she says, the members of the "white majority culture" (weiße Mehrheitsgesellschaft) have to tolerate an externally imposed designation.[4]

Although in this constellation, the point is continually made that "white" is not a biological fact—and neither does it have anything to do with skin color—but that it simply identifies a social position (whereas Black is understood to be a political self-description), it is only in the rarest of cases that individuals of Eastern or Southeastern European origin would identify themselves as Black—even if they experience racism in their daily lives. This may be motivated by a wide variety of factors. It could be because people do not want to take the risk of devaluing their experiences, since in the current anti-racist discourse they are considered to be "white." It could also be that within this anti-racist discourse, they wish to reassess their own racist body of knowledge as "white" people. Possibly, however, they also consciously identify themselves as "white" and make a distinction between such bodies of knowledge and those, for example, of refugees. Or perhaps they simply do not wish to participate in a debate over racism because they are afraid of racist experiences and are using their outward inconspicuousness as a way to evade them.

Whatever the reason, as a result of the fact that individuals of Eastern or Southeastern European origin are not able to categorize their experiences under the paradigm of Black, a portion of the racist "apparatus" is made invisible.[5] After all, there can be no doubt that these people—to follow Kien Nghi Ha's diction—are "marginalized by the dominant culture" and were historically subjected to "the violence of colonial traditions and presences." As early as 2003, Ha himself wrote about the "colonial pattern of German labor migration policies" and spoke of a "discriminatory labor migration policy as an inversion of colonial forms of expansion."[6] Thus, at a very early point in time, he transferred the postcolonial theory of the 1990s to a complicated context that extends beyond *Deutschland Schwarz Weiß* (Germany Black White).

It is impossible to comprehend why concepts of racism are currently falling back to pre-1990s status. In 1991, Stuart Hall wrote that the struggles that had arisen around the idea of Black in the United Kingdom had become problematic because they had caused the expression of other experiences to fall silent—those of Asian-British individuals, those of Black people who could not find a place for themselves in the political struggles, and those of Black women. Hall called for a new kind of "war of positions" that would acknowledge the realities and enter into the world of contradictions.[7] His claim is still valid to this day, especially for the German context. The literal adoption of critical race theory is not only based on a model of "white" and Black that is insufficient for the German context, but also on the wrong historical framework—namely, the special case of the United States of America.

This was a society that upheld slavery until 1865—that is, significantly longer than the European nations, and on its own soil, not in occupied overseas territories. At the same time, the US participated only very peripherally in colonial land grabbing; in fact, in conflicts with Europe, the nation often perceived itself to be anti-colonial. In Europe, on the other hand, colonial regimes supplanted slavery and the slave trade in the second half of the 19th century; in fact, colonialism was absurdly viewed as a kind of humanitarian intervention against the intra-African slave trade, which was controlled by Arabic traders.

Now, in the current context of anti-racism, when we speak of a postcolonial perspective and of the necessity for complete and consistent decolonization, it always seems clear exactly what we mean by *colonialism. Colonial* has become a catchall word that articulates a feeling of historical injustice toward non-Western people. In the case of the German Empire and Austria, however, it is necessary to reconstruct a historical framework that does not simply, as the Canadian historian Robert L. Nelson says, subscribe to the so-called salt water thesis: here is the motherland, there is the colony, and in between them a lot of water.[8] Portions of present-day Poland (regions with a significant Polish-speaking majority) were occupied either by Prussia or later by the German Empire for over 120 years. Following the first Congress of Berlin in 1878, which was primarily concerned with the partitioning of the Balkans, Austria-Hungary moved into Bosnia and Herzegovina and remained there for forty years—longer, that is, than the German rule in overseas regions in present-day Tanzania or Namibia. We do not describe these phenomena as colonialism. Why not? Because it was "white" people who were affected by them?

Therefore, let us ask once again: What do we mean when we use the words *postcolonial* or *decolonial*?

In the past, the term *imperialism* was commonly used to describe the will of Western European nations—particularly in the second half of the 19th century—to expand at any cost. However, this term not only described the direct, colonial seizure of lands, but countless other indirect forms of exerting influence as well.

The German Empire only entered the imperialistic competition at the time of its founding in 1871 and pushed its expansionist ambitions forward in three different directions. First of all, there was the German *Drang nach Osten* (Drive to the East)—a continuation of the Prussian territorial strategy. Prussia had acquired Polish-speaking territories following the Partitions of Poland in the 18th century (as did Austria). The integration of these provinces was never fully successful, which presented a problem for Imperial Chancellor Otto von Bismarck, since he constantly feared for the cohesion of the new empire. After its foundation, the colonial land seizure was supposed to be completed, which led him to take measures against the Polish-speaking minority: assimilation requirements, the *Kulturkampf* (culture struggle) against Catholicism, as well as displacement through settlement programs.

Second, there was overseas land seizure, which accelerated enormously in the 1880s. Nevertheless, the German Empire had entered late into the competition for overseas territories and was forced to take whatever lands had not yet been occupied. This resulted in a large colonial empire in terms of area; however, it was widely scattered and often unproductive in economic terms. With the so-called Agadir Crisis of 1911, in which Berlin attempted to reinforce its claims by deploying the gunboat SMS *Panther*, the overseas options were considered to be exhausted. Since the German Empire accepted the French occupation of Fez and Rabat, it was allowed to expand the colony of Cameroon; however, it became clear that France and England would not permit any further land grabbing. Thus, after 1911, the *Drang nach Osten* was intensified as a project for continental expansion, which was also reflected in the objectives of World War I. On the Eastern Front, the war was successful for the German Empire, so that for three years the colonial region Ober Ost was established, which extended across regions of present-day Poland, Lithuania, Latvia, and Belarus. If the German Empire had won the war, Ober Ost would undoubtedly have remained a colony.

The third expansionist thrust was directed toward Southeastern Europe, although the strategy was a more informal exertion of influence. In the period after 1911, concepts of *Mitteleuropa* (Middle Europe) had become dominant—meaning a major economic area that would be administered by Germany in cooperation with Austria. The aim was to establish an autarky with regard to raw materials, and Southeastern Europe was seen as a *Ergänzungsraum* (complimentary space) for Germany. Using a strategy of economic "penetration," military-industrial advice, and "moral conquest" through foreign cultural policy, the intention was to make both the Balkan states as well as the lurching Ottoman Empire dependent upon Germany. Particularly in economic terms, these goals were, in fact, accomplished between 1920 and 1939: during that period, the Southeastern European states carried out between a third and half of their foreign trade with the German Empire, which in this way also became the dominant factor in the region.

However, the informal strategies of domination could turn into cruder forms at any moment. This became apparent following the seizure of power by the National Socialist Party. Adolf Hitler continued the project of continental expansion, just as he had set forth in his programmatic manifesto *Mein Kampf*, albeit based on the "racially" founded concept of *Lebensraum* (living space). Thus, World War II can also be seen as a militarized attempt at colonial expansion to the east—beginning with the invasion into Poland, which had been independent since 1919. In this project, the Southeastern European states were expected to be obedient allies—which actually worked in the cases of Romania, Bulgaria, and Croatia. Less cooperative states like Serbia and Greece were subjected to harsh occupying regimes. If the Third Reich had won the war, these regions would doubtless have been caught in a colonial German *Großraumwirtschaft* (greater economic space), but as so often before, the Western powers hindered these plans.

If a critical race theory were to be applied in the German context, this context of historical injustice would have to be taken into account. The fact is that in the German case, ostensibly "white" Europeans were racialized: for example, the SS's Rasse- und Siedlungshauptamt (Race and Settlement Main Office) measured the Polish population according to "racial" criteria and categorized people on a scale from *eindeutschungsfähig* ("Germanizable") to *asozial* (asocial). These "racial" categorizations were also meant to be considered in connection with the German concept of nationality. The new version of the German Nationality Law of 1913 (which remained in place with few modifications until 2000) was completely focused on German ancestry, which in turn was fed by resentment over "inundation" from "the East" (especially by so-called ["white"] Eastern European Jews). In the interest of keeping the "blood" pure, the Nuremberg Laws particularly prohibited any "mixing"; similar measures had previously existed in overseas colonies such as German South West Africa (today Namibia).

In this respect, it seems strange that in the
annual report of the Koordinierungsstelle für
ein gesamtstädtisches Konzept zur Aufarbeitung
Berlins kolonialer Vergangenheit (Coordination
Office for a Citywide Concept to Reappraise Berlin's
Colonial Past), financed by Berlin's Senate, the
section covering "Postcolonial Legal Practice—
Decolonization of the Law" (Postkoloniale
Rechtspraxis – Dekolonisierung des Rechts) refers
exclusively to the overseas context.[9] No doubt this
overseas context has been neglected in the legal
history, but today it is imperative to reconstruct a
complete picture of Germany's imperial influence.
In this overall picture, internal homogenization
through anti-Semitism and the prevention of
immigration play an equally large role as expansion, with different settings and forms of rule. Only
this overall picture can make current expressions of
racism understandable.

Germany's postcolonial or postimperial
relationship to Eastern and Southeastern Europe
is also reflected in other phenomena, however: for
example, the removal of objects of cultural heritage
into museums of the Federal Republic. This ranges
from pieces of the Acropolis to the Pergamon Altar.
But especially relevant in this context is once again
the subject of immigration. Currently, the largest
groups of immigrants originate from Turkey and
Poland, with additional significant populations
from the former Yugoslavia and Greece. Based on
the historical backgrounds of these countries of
origin, it is appropriate to speak of postcolonial or
postimperial migration.

It is clear that imperialism also included the
pursuit of a cheap labor force—for example, to mine
coveted raw materials. Here, the forms of work
constantly fluctuated between forced and voluntary
employment, which was also evident in the policies

of the German Empire and later of the Federal Republic of Germany. The National Socialist regime set a gigantic program of forced labor in motion, using a primarily European workforce. This program began immediately after the invasion of Poland, when the employment offices entered the country mere hours after the armed forces in order to supply the German agricultural sector with Polish prisoners of war as quickly as possible.

Following the invasion of Poland, Heinrich Himmler described the "inferior" (minderwertig) population of the occupied *Generalgouvernement* as a "leaderless worker people" (führerloses Arbeitsvolk) that needed to be at the Germans' disposal for hard manual labor and therefore only required a rudimentary education: "Reading seems unnecessary to me" (Lesen halte ich nicht für erforderlich).[10] In 1941, Hitler described the Slavs at the Führer's headquarters as "a born mass of slaves that cry for a master; the question is only who the master is."[11] After the war turned to the Third Reich's disadvantage in 1942, however, the tone changed. Joseph Goebbels anticipated a defensive battle and initiated a shift in discourse "from [his] racially motivated battle of the superior German master race against the *Untermenschen* (subhumans) for the control of living space in the East to a defensive struggle by cultivated Europe against the rule of Communism."[12] In this scenario, the regime suddenly sought solidarity with its European forced laborers, leading to a situation in which the expression *Gastarbeiter* (guest workers) was used for the first time. Although it was not an official term, the phrase was employed so often that it made its way into the lexicon of "Nazi-German."[13]

When, beginning in 1955, the first recruitment contracts were drawn up, the term *Gastarbeiter* was given official status. The government displayed little memory of the past when it subjected the workers to

 THE WAY

a medical *Vorauslese* (preselection) process prior to entering the country or when they housed them in camps upon arrival—some of which had previously served as camps for forced laborers. The *Sonderzüge* (special trains) from Greece, Turkey, and Yugoslavia initially ended on Track 11 at Munich's main railway terminal. The new *Gastarbeiter* spent the waiting period before their reassignment to their respective employers in a converted underground bunker left over from the war, which could be entered directly from the aforementioned Track 11. The authorities were afraid that the sight of these men could remind the public of forced laborers and thereby reawaken an impression of a "state of war" or of a "slave trade."

Considering this history, it seems wrong to omit certain experiences from the increasingly generalized schematic of "white" and Black. The transferal of models from the US currently seems like a textbook escape from a discriminatory society; the real way out, however, would be to look at all experiences of historical injustice and present-day racism within a common frame, without denying their differences. This much is clear: being affected by racism oneself neither guarantees greater understanding of the situations of others, nor prevents one's own participation in discriminatory practices. Thirty years after Stuart Hall's statement that anti-racism must venture into the world of contradictions, in an even more complicated current situation, it makes little sense for us to fall behind this requirement.

Translated from the German by Mary Louise Dobrian

1 "'Goldene Kartoffel' 2021 für die unterirdische Debatte über 'Identitätspolitik,'" Neue deutsche Medienmacher*innen, https://neuemedienmacher.de/aktuelles/beitrag/goldene-kartoffel-2021-laudatio/, accessed January 22, 2022.

2 "[A]uf alle rassifizierten Menschen, die in unterschiedlichen Anteilen über afrikanische, asiatische, lateinamerikanische, arabische, jüdische, indigene oder pazifische Herkünfte oder Hintergründe verfügen. Er verbindet diejenigen, die durch die weiße Dominanzkultur marginalisiert sowie durch die Gewalt kolonialer Tradierungen und Präsenzen kollektiv abgewertet werden." Kien Nghi Ha, "'People of Color' als solidarisches Bündnis," *migrazine* 1 (2009), https://www.migrazine.at/artikel/people-color-als-solidarisches-bundnis, accessed January 22, 2022.

3 "Ganz einfach: Alle Schwarzen Menschen, die den politischen Begriff 'Schwarz' akzeptieren, bezeichne ich in diesem Buch als Schwarze, alle PoC, die diesen Begriff akzeptieren, als PoC."

4 Noah Sow, *Deutschland Schwarz Weiß*, rev. ed. (Norderstedt: Books on Demand, 2018), p. 35, pp. 41–42.

5 See Mark Terkessidis, *Psychologie des Rassismus* (Opladen: Westdeutscher Verlag, 1998).

6 "[D]iskriminatorischen Arbeitsmigrationspolitik als Inversion kolonialer Expansionsformen." Kien Nghi Ha, "Die kolonialen Muster deutscher Arbeitsmigrationspolitik," in *Spricht die Subalterne deutsch? Migration und postkoloniale Kritik*, ed. Hito Steyerl and Encarnación Gutiérrez Rodríguez (Münster: Unrast, 2003), pp. 56–107, here p. 64.

7 Stuart Hall, "Old and New Identities, Old and New Ethnicities," in *Culture, Globalization and the World-System: Contemporary Conditions for the Representation of Identity*, ed. Anthony D. King (Houndmills: Palgrave, 1991), pp. 41–68, here. pp. 56ff.

8 Robert L. Nelson, "Introduction: Colonialism in Europe? The Case against Salt Water," in *Germans, Poland, and Colonial Expansion to the East: 1850 through the Present*, ed. Robert L. Nelson (New York: Palgrave Macmillan, 2009), pp. 1–9.

9 Koordinierungsstelle für ein gesamtstädtisches Konzept zur Aufarbeitung Berlins kolonialer Vergangenheit, *Jahresbericht Decolonize Berlin* (Berlin: Koordinierungsstelle bei Decolonize Berlin, 2021), p. 17, https://decolonize-berlin.de/de/koordinierungsstelle/#publikationen, accessed January 12, 2022.

10 "Denkschrift Himmlers über die Behandlung der Fremdvölkischen im Osten (Mai 1940)," *Vierteljahreshefte für Zeitgeschichte* 5, no. 2 (1957): pp. 194–98, here p. 197.

11 "[E]ine geborene Sklaven-Masse, die nach dem Herrn schreit; es fragt sich nur, wer der Herr ist." Adolf Hitler, *Monologe im Führerhauptquartier 1941–1944: Die Aufzeichnungen Heinrich Heims*, ed. Werner Jochmann (Munich: Heyne 1980), p. 47.

12 "[V]on [s]einem rassistisch motivierten Kampf der überlegenen deutschen Herrenrasse gegen die 'Untermenschen' um Lebensraum im Osten zu einem Abwehrkampf des kultivierten Europas gegen die Herrschaft des Kommunismus." Ulrich Herbert: *Fremdarbeiter: Politik und Praxis*

des "Ausländer-Einsatzes" in der Kriegswirtschaft des Dritten Reiches (Bonn: Dietz, 1999), p. 278.

13 Robert Michael and Karin Doerr, *Nazi-Deutsch/Nazi-German: An English Lexicon of the Language of the Third Reich* (Westport, CT: Greenwood, 2002).

Beyond Climate Justice

Jason W. Moore

We are living through End Times. Or so we are told. The clock is running out. The climate crisis brings the apocalypse: "I am talking about the slaughter, death, and starvation of 6 billion people this century—that's what the science predicts," Roger Hallam, Extinction Rebellion's cofounder, told the BBC in the summer of 2019.[1] The statement should surprise no one with its originality or its urgency. It has been recycled endlessly since 1968. Its roots run deep, especially in the American imagination, which has shaped the world's Environmental Imaginary from its origins, and to its core. Americans love the apocalypse as no others in the modern world—perhaps because the Americans and the British have brought End Times to so many peoples in that modern world history.[2]

One or another version of the End of the World has been a staple of Environmentalism as we've known it since 1968. That year, Paul R. and Anne H. Ehrlich delivered an arresting view of the decade to come: the "Population Bomb" was exploding. "Hundreds of millions of people are going to starve to death [over the next decade] in spite of any crash programs embarked upon now."[3] We are, the Ehrlichs argued, in a state of emergency. Authoritarian measures— including compulsory abortions and forced sterilization—are necessary.[4] The authoritarian vision of emergency politics was reinforced that same year, when the biologist Garrett Hardin published "The Tragedy of the Commons"—the most influential environmental studies article ever written. Coercive measures, Hardin insisted (and the Ehrlichs agreed), must be taken to prevent an otherwise inevitable crisis.[5] Hardin and the Ehrlichs were not shy about the implications, of which anti-immigrant politics was a leading expression.[6] In an intellectual move perfectly consonant with the neoliberal turn, the mobility of labor was to be restricted. As for the mobility of capital: *that*, apparently, was beyond the remit of emergency politics. Work and working-class environmental problems were at best incidental to the New Environmentalism; at worst, workers were part of the problem.

The continuities between 1968 Environmentalism and today's Environmentalism are striking. Ideas of going "beyond politics," of apocalyptic warnings coupled with incrementalist reform, of "listening to the science," of an eternal conflict between Man and Nature fixed by "billions of years of evolution"—these unify a half century of *this* Environmentalism.[7] At all turns, such threads have been woven with an ideological material that says: whatever you do, please don't name the system! Of course, there have always been dissenters and exceptions to the dominant Environmentalism. But these have been no match for the sprawling eco-industrial complex of government ministries, think tanks, academic programs, foundation-financed NGOs, and Green parties. Even the governing metaphors are largely unchanged: yesterday's Spaceship Earth is, with only modest discursive shifts, today's Popular Anthropocene, reformulating the "limits to growth" and the disruption of "life support systems" in terms that would be readily grasped by participants in the first Earth Day (1970).[8]

There *are* differences—but in form rather than substance. Although the Ehrlichs still cling to an unabashed Populationism, new themes dominate in the 21st century. *Economic growth* and *consumption* are typically favored over imperial and ethnocentric Populationism. But these are neo-Malthusian stalking horses in their dominant forms. Growth and consumption are separated from their class dynamics, militarism, and the endless accumulation of capital.

The long arc of Malthusian thought—and its long cycle of Malthusian moments—is only superficially about "too many people."[9] It is principally about removing questions of human-initiated power and profit from the history of humans in the web of life. Poverty? Inequality? These can be explained in terms of "natural law"—and the lack of moral restraint by peasants and workers.[10] It's worth noting that such neo-Malthusianism underpinned the American New Right's demonization of the Black working class in the 1980s—"babies having babies"—even while it repudiated mainstream Environmentalism. In this mindset, war, poverty, inequality—all flow from natural law, not the conflict-riven character of capitalism's class, capital, and geopolitical relations. In the 1970s, the proximate cause—we were told—was overpopulation. Today, it's growth and overconsumption.

There's a slogan from the late 1960s that helps us counteract the learned hopelessness cultivated by big *e* Environmentalism: "The issue is not the issue." While Ehrlich's *Population Bomb* was the subject of lavish media attention, a very different figure from 1968 provides an antidote to the neo-Malthusian cosmology. When Martin Luther King Jr. turned publicly against the Vietnam War, he did so in a landmark 1967 speech at Riverside Church in New York City. It was entitled "Beyond Vietnam." *Beyond* meant everything. King was breaking with the Liberal Establishment, which saw the War as separate from the problem of racism. (He was pilloried by liberals as a consequence.) The problem, King underscored, was not merely the American war in Vietnam. Nor was the problem limited to American militarism, which had made it "the greatest purveyor of violence in the world today."[11] *The issue was not the issue.* In a synthesis that joined classical Marxism, the New Left's radical turn, and the Black Communist tradition of W. E. B. Du Bois, King formulated a first cut of the "triple evils" theory:

We must rapidly begin ... the shift from a
thing-oriented society to a person-oriented
society. When machines and computers, profit
motives and property rights, are considered more
important than people, the giant triplets of racism,
extreme materialism, and militarism are incapable
of being conquered.[12]

King did not stop there. Told to shut up and stay in
his lane, he responded acidly: "For those who are
telling me to keep my mouth shut, I can't do that. I'm
against segregation at lunch counters, and I'm not
going to segregate my moral concerns."[13] In a series
of speeches delivered the year before his death, he
argued for a revolutionary critique that was also a
revolutionary strategy. In his final address to the
Southern Christian Leadership Conference (SCLC),
in late summer 1967, he shared the parable of Jesus
and Nicodemus. The latter had come to Jesus and

wanted to know what he could do to be saved.
*Jesus didn't get bogged down in the kind of isolated
approach of what he shouldn't do.* Jesus didn't say,
Now Nicodemus, you must stop lying. He didn't
say, Nicodemus, you must stop cheating if you are
doing that. He didn't say, Nicodemus, you must not
commit adultery. He didn't say, Nicodemus, now
you must stop drinking liquor if you are doing that
excessively. *He said something altogether different,*
because Jesus realized something basic—that if a
man will lie, he will steal. And if a man will steal,
he will kill. *So instead of just getting bogged down in
one thing, Jesus looked at him and said, Nicodemus,
you must be born again.*[14]

Many of the New Environmentalists would come
to say something similar—and at the same time
very different. They would emphasize holism and

connectivity and harmony, even love. But they would
not name the system. (Those who did, like Barry
Commoner and Murray Bookchin, never gained
popular traction.) King, who had from his days in
seminary believed that "capitalism has outlived its
usefulness," was not afraid to name the system—nor
to name the specific mechanisms of capitalist
power.[15] The parable he shared with the SCLC
focused on the need to cultivate a revolutionary
imagination—the problems were not segregated; they
could not be fixed one at a time. "The whole society"
must be "born again." This required seeing how
"the problem of racism, the problem of exploitation,
and the problem of war are all tied together. These
are the triple evils that are interrelated."[16] It was
nothing short of an argument for a *triple alliance*: for
working-class justice, an end to America's forever
wars, and the abolition of the color line. It threatened
a radical coalition of the civil rights, labor, and
anti-war movements.

Today's Environmentalism owes everything to
what happened in the years immediately following
King's radical turn and his subsequent murder, likely
enabled by the American security state. Let us recall
the situation by summer 1968. Every year between
1964 and 1969 witnessed significant working-class
insurrections—"race riots" in the language of
the times—in major American cities. King's 1967
Riverside speech was followed by another "long, hot
summer," with more than 150 so-called riots. That fall,
during the October anti-war demo in Washington,
DC, William Yarborough, assistant chief of staff for
Army intelligence, thought "the empire was coming
apart at the seams."[17] Should social unrest radicalize,
there were too few reliable units at home to contain
revolt—and too few reliable units to fight the war in
Vietnam. Meanwhile, the New Left deepened the
critique of the knowledge factory initiated by Mario

Savio and the Free Speech Movement at Berkeley in 1964. In a radical shift, New Left radicals were outlining a fresh analysis of the American working class, transformed through the massive expansion of its white-collar ranks.[18] The danger was that New Left radicalism would sink its roots deep into the demographic bastion of postwar liberalism: the "professionals." Competition for these voters would shape the entirety of American neoliberal politics, unifying the Reagan-Clinton-Bush-Obama decades.

Environmentalism came to the rescue of an American ruling class beset by a legitimation crisis that, at least culturally, went far beyond the Great Depression. One or another version of the Environmental Imaginary that took shape between 1968 and 1974—*Population Bomb* Malthusianism, the Spaceship Earth imaginary focused by the iconic *Earthrise* (1968) and *Blue Marble* (1972) photographs, the insistence on virtuous civic behavior as a meaningful "politics," the notion of "natural limits"—had been around for a long time. As an imaginary—but also as a concrete practice of modern imperialism and financiers—its origins reach back to the dawn of capitalism in the century or so after 1492.[19] As a geocultural order, however, it dates from the time of Thomas Malthus, whose *First Essay* appeared in 1798.

The Popular Anthropocene—the wide-ranging "Man and Nature" conversation over the origins and development of modern environmental crisis—is the grandchild of Malthus, and a continuation of 1968 Environmentalism. Neo-Malthusianism is widely understood as an argument about population. That's part of it. But the real action lies elsewhere. It is fundamentally an ideological procedure that reframes capitalism's antagonisms as the outcome of deviations from—and adjustments to—"natural law." For Malthus, runaway social inequality in late

WA

18th-century England was the outcome of too many people and not enough nature—not enclosure and exploitation. It was no coincidence that Malthus was writing in a moment of unprecedented social revolt: Haiti and France were fundamental, but so too were Spencean protosocialism within England and Wolfe Tone's anti-colonial revolt in Ireland.

This was the first of three major Malthusian moments—the most recent of which begins in 1968. These occur in eras of worldwide revolt. They are a form of geocultural counterrevolution, as ruling classes scramble to reconstruct the "natural" character of extreme inequality and the desirability of Progress at moments of profound challenge. In Malthus's time, this was the "world revolution of the West"—dramatized by the French, Haitian, and American Revolutions, but including social revolts from Peru to Russia. A century later, Malthusianism returned, this time pivoting on eugenics and Social Darwinism. Again, it was a moment of industrialization and rising working-class power in the richest countries, who were also busily partitioning Africa. Importantly for 1968 Environmentalism, eugenics and "scientific racism" found especially fertile soil in the US, whose multiracial and multiethnic working class organized at a furious pace at the turn of the 19th century.

A third Malthusian moment—with us still in the Popular Anthropocene—crystallized after 1968. Historians tell us that Americans thronged to the New Environmentalism because they were suddenly affluent, or because *Earthrise* reminded them of their oneness with Spaceship Earth, or because of environmental disasters like the Santa Barbara oil spill and the Cuyahoga River fire in 1969. More pivotal was *The Population Bomb*. It provided a tailor-made narrative conducive to politics-as-usual. The New Environmental Imaginary was a problem with no enemies—save for "us," as cartoonist Walt Kelly's famous Pogo character made clear at the first Earth Day. That easy narrative—again, like the Anthropocene—made possible a frenzy of media coverage delivered by a propaganda machine happy to explain all the world's problems as the result of "too many people" and overconsumption. It was an attractive way to look at America's problems at a time of unprecedented legitimation crisis—and an American world order under unprecedented challenge. Environmentalism was a good palate cleanser after the Tet Offensive, urban riots, wildcat strikes, and campus revolts.

If today's Environmentalism is stuck in 1968, it's also stuck in 1798. The *first* Malthusian moment was constitutive of a geocultural order that most of us take for granted. This was centrist liberalism. Such liberalism was a "metastrategy" of bourgeois rule that assumed the normality and indeed desirability of Progress.[20] It's worth noting that the New Left foregrounded the complicity of centrist liberalism in the war machine. While the New Environmentalism seemed to reject Progress, it was a shallow rejection principally focused on individual behavior, a narrow localism, and radical-sounding generalities. After the first Earth Day, it became clear—unfortunately in relation to the war machine—that Environmentalism would have little to do with its radical contemporaries. It *ideologically* erased the New Left critique and *practically* embraced centrist liberalism as a political strategy that readily made its peace with corporate power in the 1980s.[21]

Centrist liberalism emerged in and through the first Malthusian moment, roughly in the "age of revolution" between 1789 and 1848. Over the next century, it killed two birds with one stone. Centrist liberalism "tamed" the radical impulse that stressed the right to subsistence and a fundamental overturn of capitalist relations, but also the conservative impulse to roll back the political and juridical gains made by (big and small) bourgeois strata.[22] Finally, it installed at the heart of modern politics the geo-cultural premise that it "was necessary to engage in conscious, continual, intelligent reformism," shaped by imperial states and their networks of power and privilege.[23] Among its pillars was Scientism—an ideology characterized by the continuous invocation of Good Science as the basis for understanding *and managing* social problems under capitalism.[24] Good Science established the (allegedly) value neutrality of bourgeois knowledge, mobilizing its "objective" findings to justify centrist-liberal managerialism and to discredit antisystemic movements as irrational.[25]

The relation between Big Science, Big Capital, and Big Empire is as old as capitalism. So too is the Environmental Imaginary. For previous civilizations, the notion that the web of life existed as a separate Nature apart from Civilization was, quite literally, unthinkable. Only with the rise of the capitalist world-ecology after 1492 does Nature appear as a cosmological domain separate from Civilized Man, and as a set of objects to be discovered, identified, and secured for endless capital accumulation. Nature was not merely a new "idea"; it was a strategy of power. To be called Natural—like women in early modern Europe—was to be ruthlessly dominated and devalued. Nature, in this light, had very little directly to do with the birds and the bees, forests and fields, soils and streams. Rather, Nature became everything the bourgeoisie did not want to pay for. *Man,* in this way of seeing and dominating, had practically nothing to do with humankind. After 1492, the female and pigmented human majority was relocated to Nature, the better to avoid paying them. This move had everything to do with the bourgeoisie's fantasy of itself as the bearer of Progress: Christianizing,

Civilizing, and Developmentalist in successive phases. The Environmental Imaginary was, therefore, far more than an imagination; it was a practical strategy of world power and profit.[26]

By 1945, this Environmental Imaginary—and its Scientism—crossed a threshold. Jürgen Habermas famously called it the "scientization of politics," whereby capitalism's social contradictions were increasingly converted into managerial problems amenable to "rational" governance.[27] Good Science became a pillar of American *world* hegemony. For the architects of Pax Americana,

> *the nonpolitical reputation of science was a critical political resource* … Science … [became] a critical, three-pronged weapon for waging a moral equivalent of war. First, in "man's" endless struggle against nature, technical know-how tipped the balance in favor of humanity. Second, scientific truth was derived from the universal laws of nature and so transcended political ideology. Finally, science revealed the unity in diversity of nature that made the interdependence of nations inevitable. Because natural phenomena such as river basins, ore deposits, and migratory routes paid no heed to "national boundaries," national progress depended on transnational cooperation. Science, therefore, ought to guide the integration of global society— the remaking of political geography—to match nature's "pattern of universal validity."[28]

This imperial sensibility was a key strand of the New Environmentalism's DNA. No finer expression of the problem could be found than in the first Earth Day. Earth Day was organized by the neo-Malthusian Democratic senator from Wisconsin Gaylord Nelson, whose immediate inspiration came from Paul Ehrlich and a largely discredited (because ineffective) anti-war tactic: the teach-in. By 1969, American radicals were engaging in very different tactics: building occupations, firebombing Reserve Officers' Training Corps centers, mass civil disobedience, wildcat strikes, organizing GIs against the war, and other activities that aimed to disrupt the Liberal Establishment and its war machine. As anti-war, labor, and anti-racist organizing was "leading students off the campus and into the streets," Barry Weisberg observed in 1971, "the Earth Day teach-ins proposed that students should return to their campuses and engage in orderly, rational dialogue with industry."[29]

Earth Day was more akin to a national holiday than a nationwide mobilization. Both houses of Congress adjourned for the day. In the main, the day's events were a tapestry of alternatively scientific and pious speeches woven with neo-Malthusian catastrophism and political theater. Some of the day's activities were delightfully banal: "trash-ins" in New York, bicycle rides in Eugene. Others were more creative: students organized a "die-in" to protest supersonic air travel at Boston's Logan Airport, leading to a dozen arrests. At one Earth Day event, radical folksinger Pete Seeger sang a delightful neo-Malthusian ditty: "We'll all be doublin' in 32 years."[30]

Earth Day speeches reflected that blend of radical-sounding End Times rhetoric that has been recycled ever since. A few highlighted working-class, feminist, and anti-racist themes—Rennie Davis, of Chicago 8 fame, called for a movement to "tear this capitalism down and set us free"—but these were a tiny minority.[31] More common were the politics of Denis Hayes, the Day's key organizer, whose anodyne call for "transcending traditional political boundaries" ably expressed the Day's centrist liberalism. Notwithstanding Earth Day's overlap with Lenin's birthday, Hayes's praxeology was decidedly

nonthreatening. "Proxy fights, lawsuits, demon-
strations, research, boycotts, ballots—whatever it
takes."[32] It was hardly a Green reprise of King's triple
evils. The political distance between Earth Day and
King manifested in the Day's iconic image: Pogo
gazes upon a forest filled with trash. The caption?
"We have met the enemy and he is us."[33] Here indeed
was a "cause," as President Nixon argued just three
months earlier, "beyond party and factions."[34]

The Nixonian possibilities of the New Environmentalism manifested without delay. A week after
the first Earth Day, South Vietnamese and American
forces, under Nixon's orders, rolled into Cambodia.
The invasion sparked the greatest anti-war
mobilization in American history. Over four million
students—half the American university student population—poured onto the streets of 1,350 campuses.
The University of California and California State
University systems shut down. Governors mobilized
National Guard units twenty-four times. In Ohio and
Mississippi, they opened fire on students, killing four
at Kent State and two at Jackson State University.[35]
These students *had* met the enemy. So had the
inhabitants of Indochina. Their enemies looked
remarkably similar.

The Earth Day infrastructure was nowhere to be
found in this historic moment. The inaction wasn't
from lack of awareness about ongoing ecocide.
That word, *ecocide*, had been floating around for
several years in New Left circles. Led by Students
for a Democratic Society, activists had been
protesting Dow Chemical's role in Operation Ranch
Hand—the American deployment of herbicides in
Vietnam—since 1967. They explicitly linked the "war
machine" to big capital and the knowledge factory:
the "military-industrial-academic complex."[36]

The New Environmentalism elaborated a
spectacularly partial holism. This holism directly

aligned with Pax Americana—and was therefore unable to challenge its ecocidal logic. Its iconic visual images—like *Earthrise* and *Blue Marble*—popularized Spaceship Earth metaphors, whose "life support system" trope is fundamental to the Popular Anthropocene. Like Spaceship Earth, the "earth system" is one scrubbed clean of the blood and dirt of empire, class exploitation, and racialized and gendered domination. This is *a* holism for sure. But it's one with many holes.

Let's call it the holism of the rich. Its practical consequences, just in the decade after 1968, were enormous. For the New Environmentalism, Nature was to be saved from workers, who were just as guilty as capitalists in producing "the" environmental crisis. Americans who suffered from the deadly political ecology of class exploitation were out of luck. Excluded from the New Environmentalist agenda were problems that devastated the industrial working class: Louisiana's notorious Cancer Alley, home to a robust petrochemical industry developed in the 1960s; Black Lung Disease suffered by coal miners; the poisoning of farmworkers.[37] Later, the anti-toxics movement, led by working-class women like Lois Gibbs, was similarly boxed out. The export of *these* environmental problems after 1968—the globalization of the dirtiest and most toxic industries to the Global South—was structurally deemphasized. The consequences of this deemphasis became horrifically evident in the early 1990s, as Big Green groups sabotaged grassroots environmentalist and labor opposition to the North American Free Trade Agreement (NAFTA).[38] Environmentalism, once again, was aligned with the priorities of American Empire, directly complicit in making neoliberal capitalism's socioecological hellscapes.

We have now come full circle, returning to King's essential insight: underpinning the problem of "the" environment, like racism, are the planetary relations of empire and capital. This is the enduring significance of the triple evils thesis. For King, Vietnam was not a mistake; it flowed logically from American world power and its pursuit of profitable investment opportunities. The imperial war machine was fundamentally bound to racism and class exploitation at home. A revolutionary ecological message—associated with figures like Herbert Marcuse and Murray Bookchin—could have been synthesized.[39] Indeed, King had already suggested as much in his Christmas 1967 sermon: "All life is interrelated. We are all caught in an inescapable network of mutuality, tied into a single garment of destiny. Whatever affects one destiny, affects all indirectly."[40] This is the ecological and internationalist expression of King's slogan: injustice anywhere is a threat to justice everywhere.

As Earth Day's organizers and other Environmentalists sat on their hands during the invasion of Cambodia and that May's extraordinary revolt, they established a precedent—one that has shaped their failure to slow, much less halt, the capitalogenic drive to the planetary inferno. They drew the worst lesson possible: American military intervention was not environmental. The disconnect between the New Left and post-1968 Environmentalism was not simply "radicalism" and "liberalism"; it was bound to different, and unbridgeable, assessments of world power as the chief threat to planetary life.

After its "golden age" in the 1970s, the New Environmentalism remained on the sidelines of domestic opposition to America's forever wars. In hindsight, Big Green's support for NAFTA was foreseeable. It had supported the New Democratic turn, led by pro-war figures like Clinton and Gore, the latter famous for 1992's *Earth in the Balance*.[41] Al Gore was a pro-war Democrat and an early adopter of regime change politics. The Environmentalist silence on imperialist

THE WAY

war had, as we've seen, been established on the first Earth Day and the invasion of Cambodia. With the first Gulf War—"By God," George H. W. Bush proclaimed that March, "we've kicked the Vietnam syndrome once and for all"[42]—the silence became deafening. (Only Greenpeace, among the major nationals, organized against the first Iraq War.)

As the US recovered from the "Vietnam syndrome" in the 1980s, Environmentalism had little to say about war, empire, and exploitation. The implications for contemporary Environmentalism are enormous. Conservation has become militarized across the Global South. Environmentalist luminaries call for new rounds of enclosure—as in E. O. Wilson's "Half-Earth," necessary to "save" the diversity of life.[43] Others, like James Lovelock, advocate the militarization of borders against dark-skinned immigrant workers—a position that has long haunted Environmentalism in the rich countries (see 1972's *Blueprint for Survival*).[44] Since 2001, the Anthropocene's popularity has reinforced this tendency. Its framing of planetary crisis removes from consideration the greatest threats to human and planetary well-being: capitalogenic climate change, financialization, and the militarized accumulation that makes the whole shit show possible. Such reckonings greenwash the dystopian movements of America's forever wars and wildly proliferating climate violence since 2002.

If we wonder why Environmentalism hasn't done anything to slow capitalism's rush to the planetary inferno, there's a good reason for that. It was never *supposed* to do anything. For all the talk about an environmentalist revolution in values—living simply, recycling, going organic, sacralizing dietary preferences—their political impact was always exceedingly marginal. At best it was a "march through the institutions"—law, big NGOs, regulatory agencies,

OUT

and, sometimes, political parties—by which boomer
professionals came to manage environmental
problems. By the 1980s, the New Environmentalism
was increasingly in explicit alliance with corporate
power and the pursuit of market-oriented solutions.
Challengers have emerged since then—often
narrated as Environmental Justice movements—but
the basic tendency is unbroken.

What, then, is the radical way out of the climate
crisis? I have no stone tablets with the Truth etched
upon them. But all of us have access to *history*—the
history of liberation movements, the history of
Environmentalism, the history of capitalism. Among
the great tragedies of the post-1968 Environmental
Imaginary has been the marginalization of a radical
historical imagination—one that might grasp the
interrelated history of power, profit, and life in the
modern world.

Among its consequences, as we've seen, is the
hegemony of a Whole Earth holism—the holism of
the rich—that pits Man against Nature. The argument
that "the" environmental crisis stems from Man's
violation of "natural law"—a thesis that runs in a
direct line from Malthus to the Anthropocene—has
been an ideological hammer in the hands of Empire
and Capital for the past two centuries. Underneath
it is a bloody and violent history of profit-seeking
imperialism that stretches back to 1492. From the 17th
century onward, Civilizing Projects redefined Nature
as everything the bourgeoisie did not wish to pay for,
and relocated the vast majority of humankind into
the realm of Nature—the better to cheapen them and
to convert their lives and labor into capital. Neither
Man nor Nature are innocent descriptions here, a
reality that comes into focus only once we understand that capitalism is not merely an economic and
political system, but a mode of thought and ideology
that redefines the contradictions of power, profit,

and life as collisions between Man and Nature. This
is the history of successive Malthusian moments.
In such a scheme, the task of Civilization was to
manage the problems of Nature, which included the
vast majority of humans, variously un-Christian,
un-Civilized, and un-Developed. Today's Sustainable
Development complex—well-financed by governments and Foundations—is but the latest expression
of this long history.

The radical response since the 1990s has
emphasized a laundry list diagnosis of the planetary
crisis—race, gender, sexuality, indigeneity, environmentalism, and much beyond. All are crucial. The
problem is that what binds their concrete interrelations is rarely specified, their historical development
unexplored. The result is a democratic theory of
causation in which "everything is connected to
everything." True enough, up to a point. But such
connections are never equal, and effective radical
politics involves exploiting the asymmetries: the
weak links. Their asymmetries change in relation to
the movement of the whole. And there's the rub, not
just in assessing the Problem, but in forging a revolutionary politics of planetary justice. World history
is indispensable because it tells us clearly that the
history of civilizations is a history of humans *in* the
web of life, actively making webs of life even as they
are shaped *by* webs of life.[45] Viewed in this light, the
history of class society is a history of asymmetries,
producing and produced by webs of life. The genius
of Marx and Engels was to understand how the
very processes of domination and exploitation
that created modern working classes—far more
heterogenous than most Marxists admit—were those
that would allow for the liberation of "the soil and
the worker."[46]

It is here that we can return to King, the triple evils
thesis, and the parable of Nicodemus. The issue was

not the issue. Why? Because for King "the triple evils
… are interrelated." They are problems of the "whole
society."[47] Militarism, racism, and class exploitation
are problems of the "whole society": of capitalism
as a whole. Just as Vietnam was a symptom of a
deeper pathology that extended beyond American
militarism, the climate crisis runs far beyond
atmospheric carbonization and increasingly volatile
weather. King refused to construct a laundry list of
problems. Adding up was not sufficient. Militarism,
racism, and exploitation: each was strategically
related to the others; their world-historical meaning
emerges through their interrelations. This is why I
have taken to insisting that we move beyond climate
justice. We must carry forth a message of a *concretely*
interrelated climate crisis born of capitalism as a
world-ecology of power, profit, and life five centuries
ago. We live in the *Capitalocene*—the "age of
capital"—not the Anthropocene.[48]

Atmospheric carbonization and the resulting
demise of Holocene climatic stability must be
situated geohistorically. To use the descriptive
categories of the One Percent—abstract markets,
population movements, or technologies—is to
doom one's strategy from the start. Rather, we can
make sense of planetary crisis as one in which
the geophysical dimensions of climate change are
fundamentally bound to the Capitalocene's trinity:
climate class divide, climate patriarchy, and climate
apartheid.[49] Such a historical perspective intimately
informs socialist strategy in the planetary inferno,
as we come to understand that capitalogenic trinity
as the *cause*, and not only the consequence, of the
climate crisis.

At every turn, we can move beyond Pogo's
lament—"We have met the enemy and he is us"—and
prioritize the *specific* political, economic, and cultural
agents of capitalogenic climate change. It's not Man,

but *Capital*, that is responsible for the planetary inferno. As the radical folk singer Utah Phillips liked to remind his audiences: "They have names and addresses."[50] The guilty can be held accountable for their crimes, and planetary justice delivered. The "whole society" with and within the web of life can be reinvented as if "all life is interrelated"—as if "we are all caught in an inescapable network of mutuality, tied into a single garment of destiny."[51]

1   "'Something Drastic Has to Happen' Roger Hallam | BBC HardTalk | Extinction Rebellion," YouTube video, 24:37, August 17, 2019, https://www.youtube.com/watch?v=9HyaxctatdA&t=993s, accessed January 4, 2021.

2   Betsy Hartmann, *The America Syndrome: Apocalypse, War, and Our Call to Greatness* (San Francisco: Seven Stories, 2017).

3   Paul R. Ehrlich [and Anne H. Ehrlich, uncredited], *The Population Bomb* (New York: Ballantine, 1968), p. xi.

4   Paul R. Ehrlich and Anne H. Ehrlich, *Population, Resources, Environment*, 2nd ed. (San Francisco: W. H. Freeman, 1972), p. 372.

5   Garrett Hardin, "The Tragedy of the Commons," *Science* 162 (1968): pp. 1243–48.

6   Crystallized a decade later, in Paul R. Ehrlich, Loy Bilderback, and Anne H. Ehrlich, *The Golden Door: International Migration, Mexico, and the United States* (New York: Ballantine, 1979), but on display as early as 1972: Edward Goldsmith et al., "A Blueprint for Survival," *The Ecologist* 2, no. 1 (1972): pp. 2–43.

7   The first two quotations are slogans of Extinction Rebellion, covered effectively by Colin Kinniburgh, "Can Extinction Rebellion Survive?" *Dissent* 67, no. 1 (2020): pp. 125–33; "billions of years" is from Ehrlich, *The Population Bomb* (see note 3), p. 29.

8   See respectively R. Buckminster Fuller, *Operating Manual for Spaceship Earth* (Carbondale, IL: Southern Illinois University Press, 1969); Donella H. Meadows et al., *The Limits to Growth* (New York: Universe, 1972); Jason W. Moore, "Confronting the Popular Anthropocene," *New Geographies* 9 (2017): pp. 186–91.

9   Thomas R. Robertson, *The Malthusian Moment* (New Brunswick: Rutgers University Press, 2012); quotation from Ehrlich, *The Population Bomb* (see note 3), p. 17.

10   David McNally, *Against the Market* (London: Verso, 1993).

11   Martin Luther King Jr., "Beyond Vietnam: A Time to Break the Silence," public lecture, Riverside Church, New York, April 4, 1967, https://wilpfus.org/sites/default/files/docs/5-MLK-Beyond-Vietnam-speech-in-sections.pdf, accessed January 5, 2022.

12   Ibid.; W. E. B. Du Bois, *Black Reconstruction in America 1860–1880* (New York: Atheneum, 1935).

13   Martin Luther King Jr., "America's Chief Moral Dilemma," public lecture, Hungry Club Forum, Atlanta, May 10, 1967, https://www.youtube.com/watch?v=IAYGYmXOAyg, accessed January 2, 2022.

14   Martin Luther King Jr., "Where Do We Go from Here?," in *A Testament of Hope*, ed. James Melvin Washington (New York: Harper & Row, 1986), pp. 245–52, here pp. 250–51.

15   Martin Luther King Jr., "To Coretta Scott," letter, July 18, 1952, https://kinginstitute.stanford.edu/king-papers/documents/coretta-scott, accessed January 3, 2022.

16   King, "Where Do We Go from Here?" (see note 14).

17   Quoted in Alexander Cockburn, *The Golden Age Is in Us: Journeys and Encounters 1987–1994* (London: Verso, 1996), p. 325.

18   See especially David Gilbert, Robert Gottlieb, and Gerry Tenney, "The 'Port Authority Statement' (1967)," in *Revolutionary Youth & the New Working Class*, ed. Carl Davidson (Pittsburgh: Changemaker, 2011), pp. 52–127.

19   Jason W. Moore, "Opiates of the

Environmentalists? Anthropocene Illusions, Planetary Management & the Capitalocene Alternative," *Abstrakt* (November 2021), http://www.abstraktdergi.net/opiates-of-the-environmentalists-anthropocene-illusions-planetary-management--the-capitalocene-alternative/, accessed December 21, 2021.

20 Immanuel Wallerstein, *The Modern World-System IV: Centrist Liberalism Triumphant, 1789–1914* (Berkeley: University of California Press, 2011), p. 5.

21 Mark Dowie, *Losing Ground: American Environmentalism at the Close of the Twentieth Century* (Cambridge, MA: MIT Press, 1996).

22 Wallerstein, *The Modern World-System IV* (see note 20), p. xvi.

23 Ibid., p. 6.

24 Ariel Salleh, "Neoliberalism, Scientism and Earth System Governance," in *The International Handbook of Political Ecology*, ed. Raymond L. Bryant (New York: Edward Elgar, 2015), pp. 432–46.

25 Moore, "Opiates of the Environmentalists?" (see note 19).

26 Raj Patel and Jason W. Moore, *A History of the World in Seven Cheap Things* (Berkeley: University of California Press, 2018).

27 Jürgen Habermas, *Toward a Rational Society* (Cambridge, UK: Polity, 1987), pp. 61–80.

28 Perrin Selcer, *The Postwar Origins of the Global Environment: How the United Nations Built Spaceship Earth* (New York: Columbia University Press, 2018), pp. 6–7.

29 Barry Weisberg, *Beyond Repair* (Boston: Beacon Press, 1971), p. 31.

30 Robertson, *The Malthusian Moment* (see note 9), p. 170.

31 Rennie Davis, "Up Agnew Country," in *Earth Day—The Beginning: A Guide to Survival*, ed. National Staff of Environmental Action (New York: Bantam, 1970), pp. 87–88, here p. 88.

32 Denis Hayes, "The Beginning," in ibid., pp. xiii–xv, here p. xv.

33 Finis Dunaway, "Gas Masks, Pogo, and the Ecological Indian: Earth Day and the Visual Politics of American Environmentalism," *American Quarterly* 60, no. 1 (2008): pp. 67–99.

34 Richard M. Nixon, "Annual Message to the Congress on the State of the Union," January 22, 1970, https://www.presidency.ucsb.edu/documents/annual-message-the-congress-the-state-the-union-2, accessed January 3, 2022.

35 Kirkpatrick Sale, *SDS* (New York: Vintage, 1973), p. 445.

36 J. William Fulbright, "The War and Its Effects: The Military-Industrial-Academic Complex," in *Super-State: Readings in the Military-Industrial Complex*, ed. Herbert I. Schiller (Urbana, IL: University of Illinois Press, 1970), pp. 171–78; Sale, *SDS* (see note 35).

37 Chad Montrie, *A People's History of Environmentalism in the United States* (London: Continuum, 2011).

38 Dowie, *Losing Ground* (see note 21).

39 Herbert Marcuse, "Ecology and Revolution," *Liberation* 16 (1970): pp. 10–12; Murray Bookchin, *Post-Scarcity Anarchism* (Berkeley: Ramparts, 1970).

40 Martin Luther King Jr., "Christmas Sermon on Peace and Nonviolence," Ebenezer Baptist Church, Atlanta, December 24, 1967, https://www.organism.earth/library/document/christmas-sermon-on-peace-and-nonviolence, accessed January 10, 2022.

41 Al Gore, *Earth in the Balance: Ecology and the Human Spirit* (New York: Houghton Mifflin, 1992).

OUT

42 George H. W. Bush, "Remarks
to the American Legislative
Exchange Council," March 1, 1991,
https://www.govinfo.gov/content/
pkg/PPP-1991-book1/html/
PPP-1991-book1-doc-pg195-2.
htm, accessed January 3, 2022.

43 Edward O. Wilson, *Half-Earth:
Our Planet's Fight for Life* (New
York: W. W. Norton, 2016).

44 John Ingham, "Plea for a Bigger
Navy to Keep Out Climate
Immigration," *The Express*,
May 31, 2010, https://www.
express.co.uk/news/uk/178199/
Plea-for-a-bigger-Navy-to-
keep-out-climate-immigration,
accessed January 2, 2022.

45 Jason W. Moore, *Capitalism in the
Web of Life* (London: Verso, 2015).

46 Karl Marx, *Capital* (New York:
Vintage, 1977), p. 638; Jason
W. Moore, "Das planetare
Proletariat im planetaren
Inferno," *LfB: Literaturforum im
Brecht-Haus* 7 (2021): pp. 4–11.

47 King, "Where Do We Go from
Here?" (see note 14).

48 Jason W. Moore, ed.,
Anthropocene or Capitalocene?
(Oakland: PM Press, 2016).

49 Jason W. Moore, "The
Capitalocene and
Planetary Justice," *Maize*
6 (2019): pp. 49–54.

50 Quoted in Naomi Klein, *No Logo*
(New York: Knopf, 2000), p. 325.

51 King, "Christmas Sermon"
(see note 40).

The Way
Out of
Bad Sex

Katherine
Angel

WAY

In 2009, twenty-four-year-old Vincent Glad set up a
Facebook group called the Ligue du LOL. The journalists in the group, many of them emerging from the
prestigious and selective *grandes écoles* that furnish
French public life with bright young minds, targeted
in their activities other journalists and public figures,
mostly women, people of color, and gay or bisexual
men. Feminist Daria Marx was sent death and rape
threats. The group photoshopped her face onto por-
nographic imagery and widely circulated it. A male
journalist's blog about mental health and anxiety
was ridiculed, instigating online pile-ons. A Jewish
blogger whose mother had died was photoshopped
with a swastika tattoo on his chest. Science writer
Florence Porcel was pranked via a fake job interview
over the telephone, which was then circulated online.
Many people spoke of having been driven to suicidal
thoughts by these tricks. Blogger Capucine Piot
unwittingly dated one of the members, who pranked
her by telling her that he might have HIV; it was
untrue. LOL!

The Ligue du LOL's activities slowed down in 2013.
As Marie Le Conte put it in the *New Statesman*, this
was understandable, since "by that point, they were
getting busier" with their careers.[1] Members were
rising in the ranks of magazines and newspapers,
often in left-leaning, hip publications such as
Libération, *Les Inrockuptibles*, and *Slate*.

It's hard not to see this targeting of women and
minorities, in a still shockingly white line of work, as
a policing of entry to the profession. "Entering the
professions" is a phrase used by Virginia Woolf in
Three Guineas, published in 1938, as debates intensified over whether war with Germany was justified.
Three Guineas was a response to a letter from a man
asking Woolf how, in her opinion, and as a woman,
war can be prevented. Woolf uses the letter to stage
a debate between pacifism and war, and crucially

she links this question to that of women's position in society. She makes the case—much derided in her day—that the tyranny of the patriarchal state and the tyranny of the fascist state are one and the same. Addressing the men who want women's support in fighting the fascist, she notes that the fascist is now "interfering with *your* liberty"; "you are feeling in your own persons what your mothers felt when they were shut out."[2]

Woolf prickles at being asked as a woman to "join" the fight against fascism. She underlines the fact that women have been working for men—doing unpaid work, sacrificing their earnings to Arthur's Education Fund (the money families were happy to set aside for boys' education at the expense of girls' education)—for centuries. When women are told by men that they are fighting to protect "our country," she asks herself: "What does 'our country' mean to me an outsider?" How much, she asks, of England in fact belongs to a woman? "Her sex and class has very little to thank England for in the past." The outsider, she writes, will say that "as a woman, I have no country. As a woman I want no country. As a woman my country is the whole world."[3]

Three Guineas is a fascinating text; circumlocutory, evasive, slippery, it is both angrier than *A Room of One's Own* (1929) and more anxious about that anger. A lot of the work is done in footnotes, unusually for Woolf. It's also problematic, since it takes for granted the question of class: the text is about "the daughters of educated men" who are "entering the professions" (law, medicine, journalism).[4] And the easy universalism of her statements is questionable in a world riven by inequalities among women themselves. But Woolf is also adamant and clear-sighted about the link between money and power. She was fascinated by money (her diaries are peppered with delighted recordings of the money that she earned, herself, by

her pen), and one of her arguments for the right of
women to work is in fact her understanding of the
power of labor strikes. In the essay, she argues for
equal pay, and for wages for housework and parent-
ing. Woolf understood, more than many members of
her upper-class cadre, quite what money could mean
and enable, quite what oppressive structures it could
free one from.

Woolf is deeply uncomfortable about joining
the society that has excluded her. Describing an
imagined procession of the sons of educated men, in
all their garb and finery (Woolf is also obsessed with
clothes and what they signify), she writes: "We have
to ask ourselves, here and now, do we wish to join
that procession, or don't we? On what terms shall we
join that procession? Above all, where is it leading us,
the procession of educated men?"[5]

Professions, she argues, have an undeniable effect
upon the professors. They make the people who
practice them possessive, jealous of any infringement
of their rights, and highly combative if anyone dares
dispute them. Are we not right, then, in thinking that
if we enter the same professions we shall acquire the
same qualities? And "do not such qualities lead to
war?" How, asks Woolf, can the daughters of educated
men, leaving "the private house, with its nullity, its
immorality, its hypocrisy, its servility," enter the
professions and yet "remain civilized human beings;
human beings, that is, who wish to prevent war?"[6]

Reading *Three Guineas* again recently, I was struck
by its uncanny resonance with our contemporary
conversations about harassment and abuses of power
in the workplace. Like Woolf, I too feel ambivalence
about joining institutions that have proved themselves
such fertile grounds for the exclusion of women, and
for their abuse. How can we, now, enter the professions and yet remain civilized human beings, human
beings who wish to prevent abuse? The question, as

Woolf puts it, is how to "join the professions and yet remain uncontaminated by them."[7]

I do not only mean this literally—though plenty of women have precisely this experience, of entering a profession and having to choose between aligning themselves with its (male-dominated, often sexist) values or sidelining themselves from the center of the action. I also mean it symbolically, in relation to the concepts that we use. In our attempts, as women, to take up the space that has so often been denied to us, must we inevitably end up adopting the values of the space we are entering? How can we take up that space without being "contaminated" by it? This is, in part, the question that motivated my recent book, *Tomorrow Sex Will Be Good Again*:[8] how to conceive of a better sexual world for women, without insisting that women's sexuality be a certain way—in particular, without insisting that women's sexuality must itself be able to ward off the violence and coercion that is so pervasive in women's experience of sex. How can women be safe from violence and experience greater pleasure, without insisting, also, that women's sexuality be like men's (or be as men's is assumed to be), without insisting that women adopt, in their sexuality and their personhood, the values associated—rightly or wrongly—with men and theirs?

Bill Cosby gave Quaaludes to women he wanted to have sex with.[9] Or perhaps we should use the phrase "to rape" rather than "to have sex with." In denying his intention to rape, he can easily be considered simply to be lying, verbally misrepresenting what he knows to have been his true intentions. But it might be inaccurate to say that Cosby knew he was committing rape. It's possible that Cosby, like countless men, genuinely—sincerely—believed that he wasn't committing rape. And it doesn't help the conversation about sexual violence against women to deny

this, as perverse and counterintuitive as it may sound
to us. We need to rethink our understandings of what
"genuine" and "sincere" mean; not because people
lie (though they do), but because they fail to have
self-knowledge—a failure that can of course be linked
to power, and to an "epistemology of ignorance,"
to use Charles W. Mills's phrase, which refers to a
form of unknowing or non-knowing that supports
inequality.[10] Shannon Sullivan and Nancy Tuana
summarize this concept in this way: "Sometimes
what we do not know is not a mere gap in knowledge,
the accidental result of an epistemological oversight.
… [A] lack of knowledge or an unlearning of something previously known often is actively produced
for purposes of domination and exploitation."[11] The
enraged umbrage that men can take when accused
of rape, assault, or coercion of many forms (or in fact
of any wielding of their power)—or the hurt anger
that many men can voice in a conversation about this
question—emerges from a profound confusion not
only about what rape is, but what sex is. The sincere,
deeply convinced assertion of innocence—and of
outrage under accusation—in men is an indication
that what we need to talk about isn't just what counts
as rape, but what counts as sex.

For many men, sex is something men do *to*
women. Politician George Galloway, commenting on
the allegations against Julian Assange, said that one
of the women had had consensual sex with Assange,
after which she "woke up to him having sex with
her again. This is something which can happen, you
know." Note the passive construction here, that while
seeing sex as something that is done to women by
men, also simultaneously sidesteps any agency or
responsibility on the part of the man. "Not everybody
needs to be asked prior to each insertion," Galloway
said, as well as claiming that while it might be "sordid
and bad sexual etiquette" not to have "tapped her on

the shoulder and said: 'Do you mind if I do it again?,'"
to describe this situation of "bad manners" as rape is
to "bankrupt the term rape of all meaning."[12]

At the root of this shockingly blithe account is not
simply a retrograde view of what counts as rape, but
a depressingly unambitious, and essentially coercive,
view of what counts as sex. If sex is something a man
does to a woman's body ("if I do it again"—the man
is active, the woman acted upon)—something to
which she may or may not consent, often, it seems,
unenthusiastically—then, once a woman has agreed
to it being done to her, the conversation is over. But
not only is this model of sex utterly joyless and
depressing—one senses that Galloway's experience is
of having to ask women to endure his insertions and
doings—it is also very dangerous, precisely because
to rule out pleasure is dangerous. It forecloses the
possibility of sex being something to which women
might not just consent, but in fact actively desire and
welcome; it doesn't even entertain the possibility
of a mutually enthusiastic activity, where doing is
shared. Sex is an object to be acquired, rather than an
activity to be undertaken together. This foreclosure
raises the all too inevitable possibility that women
who *do* actively, enthusiastically pursue and enjoy
sex are relegated to an inferior category of woman,
who can legitimately be scorned and shunned and
pitied (except when they can be instrumentally
enjoyed for precisely their desirousness) and are
therefore rendered vulnerable to violence on that
account. And it also resigns itself to sex as a purely
passive activity for women: one where we endure,
allow, suffer the desires of men—and where, once we
have given our unambitious, resigned consent, we
have no grounds for refusing a further "insertion," a
further anything.

This is why emphasizing women's ability to
actively desire—allowing them sexual hunger,

appetite, need, drive, longing, pleasure, acquisitiveness—and allowing them indeed to ask for sex, is so important. Because only when women can enthusiastically say yes to sex can we raise the bar for what men are entitled to expect. A silent acquiescence, an absence of "no" will no longer be a legitimate background condition to their wielding their greater physical and social power over us. If women can't be seen to want sex, they can't be seen to actively refuse either. If we are always these long-suffering objects of insertion, then how are men—especially those with the sexual entitlement of a Bill Cosby or the bullish tone-deafness of a George Galloway—to tell between an instance of indifferent, or demure acquiescence and a silent suffering of coercion? There may be a vested interest, that is, in not being able to tell what a woman wants. This might be why women's active desire is threatening—because if you can enthusiastically say yes, you can also enthusiastically say no and reject a man. If men are to understand the ways in which they coerce women—if they are to develop an understanding of rape—they need a different model of sex.

There are many reasons, then, to want to define women's sexuality in terms that enable us to repel male violence. Violence abounds, but not just violence: bad, disappointing, humiliating, painful, unhappy sex. And it has been a temptation to define women's sexuality as the assertive, willful, acquisitive, lustful, confident thing we associate with male sexuality. If we are to be emancipated, after all—if we are to expect good sex—and if we are to be the liberated women we want to be, we must align ourselves with this emphatic version of desire. We must speak our desire loudly—and therefore know it in the first place. This is why models of women's sexuality that privilege a gutsy—dare I say ballsy?—performance of desire, are so appealing to us (while

they also often disgust and disconcert us). They hold
out the prospect of protecting women by matching
the power of men. They hold out a vision of strength,
of force; they promise an ability to resist the shaming
forces of a misogynistic world. This woman will not
buckle, they whisper tantalizingly.

And yet women's desire has also long been seen as
inhabiting a precarious position, constantly at risk of
tipping over into either voraciousness and promiscu-
ity, or into indifference. Our hopes for female desire
veer wildly between a vision of lustful entitlement
(finally, we'll beat the men at their game, or at least
join them!) and an insistence on its elusiveness.
Research in recent years has shown that women may
say they are not aroused by something when their
bodies in fact show signs of physiological arousal
(this is called nonconcordance). (Much gleeful media
commentary has ensued, often making the fallacious
leap to saying that this physiological arousal is a
window onto desire—something the researchers
themselves clearly do not suggest.)

The status of physiological arousal is complex and,
I would argue, ambiguous. There's a scene in Lena
Dunham's *Girls* in which Marnie meets a young art
star. He's short, arrogant, famous. They're standing
outside a bar, not quite flirting; it's awkward—he's full
of himself, she's ambivalently awed. The conversation
jerks along. And then he leans over and says to her,
in a tone laced with threat and with enjoyment of
its own power: "I want you to know: the first time
I fuck you, I might scare you a little. Because I'm
a man, and I know how to do things." She's angry,
outraged. She storms back into the bar, goes into the
bathroom, locks the door behind her, and begins to
masturbate.[13]

I was taken aback by this scene, but I was not
unhappy to see something so complex portrayed
on screen—I was pleased that Dunham had dared

to go here. It differed from the kind of scene one
sometimes sees in films, of men being creeps and
women being overcome by their charm, their
unmistakable worth. It wasn't a scene that encouraged you to think that women fall for arseholes. It
was a scene that showed you that what is shocking,
problematic, and uncomfortable can sometimes
be arousing. This can be utterly confounding for
women; it's confusing to feel physiological arousal
in relation to something that one might object to (in
this case, a man's invocation of fear). It doesn't, in fact,
follow from physiological arousal that women *want*
anything in particular, or that men should overrule
what women say—no matter what misogynists
and rape apologists might say. We need, don't we, to
allow space for the uncomfortable and inconvenient
aspects of sexuality too.

Commentators do make leaps, however. Brooke
Magnanti wrote that "the difference between what
women report is turning them on and what is
actually getting their bodies to respond, is significant.
*We may think we know what turns people on, but the
data are giving researchers a very different picture.*"[14]
She assumes here that "data" amounts to physiological evidence, and that people's subjective reports
about sex do not count as data: what is self-reported,
in other words, is not data.

The powerful idea that only what is externally
measurable and visible is legitimate—along with
the equivalency between physiological and sexual
arousal—has worrisome effects, and trades on the
slippery ways in which the terms "objective" and
"subjective" are used. Writers in this field now
routinely distinguish between "objective" arousal
(the arousal evidenced through, for example, blood
flow measurements) and "subjective" arousal (what
women say they find arousing). But these terms are
being used in two different ways. "Objective" is being

used to mean visualizable and verifiable by others, and "subjective" to mean felt or experienced. There is a second sense, however, in which "objective" is used to mean true, and "subjective" to mean unreliable, misleading, potentially untruthful. The one usage does not follow from the other; what is subjective in the sense of being personally felt rather than verifiable is not necessarily, by that token, misleading or untrue. To use these senses interchangeably involves *assuming* that what is subjective (in the sense of being personal, felt, experienced) is by definition unreliable, and of problematic epistemological status.

The more honest formulation would be "physiological" evidence contrasted with "self-reported" evidence. To assume that "self-reported" is "subjective"—and to assume that what is self-reported is discountable—already loads the dice, especially given that the term "subjective" is usually used in contrast to "objective," and that "objective" is a highly valorized, even overprivileged ideal in rhetoric about science. This usage indicates to the reader that there is something less valuable, less reliable, less important about the self-reports women are giving in these accounts. Using these terms in this way builds in a presumption that physiological arousal is the true index of arousal (and perhaps desire), and that subjective, self-reported arousal (what women say) is fundamentally to be mistrusted. In other words, it primes us to believe something is being demonstrated, in argument, that is in fact merely being assumed: that the body's evidence trumps a woman's feeling.

Scientific research into sexuality is often full of paraphernalia; it hopes to lure sexuality into a neutral space, shed its cultural trappings, and reveal its workings under the bright lights and technical instruments of the laboratory. Countless studies investigate the workings of women's physiological arousal and its mapping (or not) onto their statements about sexuality. The picture that can emerge from these studies—and the bewilderment and fascination with nonconcordance—suggests, if one wants to see it that way, that women are, in any case, sexually unknowable to themselves. Their true desires are capricious, and buried. Sexual desire, just like woman herself, is fickle, volatile, and—also just like a woman—is to be courted, chased, hunted, treated with deft but entirely strategic and goal-oriented, acquisitive means; with various technologies intent on seeking out the truth. Desire itself is contradictory, perplexing, and men are left to do delicate and brutal detective work.

There is, in fact, an uncanny affinity between this model of sexual desire in women and the premises on which the male pick-up artist relies. This fickle prize (desire in women, or women themselves) is to be played, strategically managed, hunted down. Ryan Gosling, in *Crazy, Stupid, Love*, is an expert on women, a master of seduction. He has a strategy, and it works every time. He takes pity on a middle-aged male, depressed and separated from his wife, and advises him to man up and get some action. He coaches the older man, whose hit rate begins to soar. The creepily incestuous twist to the plot is that Ryan begins to date the older man's daughter; the specter at the feast is the paternal figure becoming blurred with the younger man. Is the girl's father becoming her lover? Standing naked, glorious, in a gym changing room, hovering over his intimidated, podgy protégé, Gosling places one confident foot on a bench, his tackle at the other man's head height—of course we, the viewers, don't see it; the comedy lies in its obscuring—and says, in delighted triumph: "The war of the sexes is over, and we won."[15]

Nonconcordance is an inconvenient phenomenon (though it's one that I suggest, in *Tomorrow Sex*

Will Be Good Again, is a measurement artifact: a
result of our misconceptions of how sexuality can
in fact be studied). Sexuality is, regardless, rife with
contradictions, ambiguity, confusion. We are opaque
to ourselves, and therefore also to others. There are
no easy solutions, no simple ways out. But I want to
conclude with two claims. First, that by all too often
placing the burden on women to know and declaim
their desire, we might be requiring them to resolve
the cultural problems around pleasure and power
whose responsibility they should not solely bear.
The injunction to know and express your desire,
as a measure to foreclose rape, is a heavy burden
to bear. In fact, the emphasis on an enthusiastic,
active yes—the obligation to it, we might say—faces
this particular difficulty: we might not know in
advance what we want; sometimes we want things
in response to a particular person, a particular body,
a particular time. Desire emerges in relation. And
so the emphasis on—the fetishization of—assertive,
loud, defiant desire in women can obscure the much
more tender, fraught negotiation of what is unknown
that is part and parcel of sexuality. And it's precisely
the uncertain, unclear space between yes and no that
we need to learn to discuss and navigate. Perhaps we
shouldn't work backward from assumed knowledge;
we should work forward from curiosity.

Second, we are also asking *sexuality* itself to
bear this burden; trying to seek a model of desire
that will ward off violence. It can never do this. It's
tempting to think that our models of desire should
not contain this vulnerability to male violence. But
how sexuality works in women should not be seen
as potentially offering grounds for women's violation,
or for insuring against it. Making our understanding
of female sexuality, of any sexuality, defer to the
potential for violence, is buckling, at an epistemological level, to the moral universe of misogyny and

sexism, in which our nonautonomy is presumed.
It involves deferring to the idea that in the complex
space of vulnerability and openness to the other, and
of engagement with one's own sometimes unknown
desire, lies a moral weakness that we must keep at
bay in order to avert male violence. Yet denying that
space and its riches and risks does nothing to counter
male violence. We need an ethics of that space, not a
model of desire that will deny it. There are men who
don't know how to gauge desire in others, and how
to calibrate theirs with another. There are men who
feel entitled, and also unconfident. There are men
who lunge, who grope, who mistake insistence for
playfulness. There are men who feel most aggrieved
when the power at work in their capacity to blur
consent and nonconsent is pointed out to them.
But just because it's not an alleyway scenario, a
knifepoint assault, and just because the rest of the
time was consensual, doesn't mean it's not an abuse
of some kind. Rebecca Traister, Christina Tesoro, and
Melissa Febos, among many others, have over the
past few years urged that, instead of asking "did you/
she say yes?" we should be asking instead what forms
of power are operating in the room.[16] We should also
be asking what kinds of desire are operating in the
room—and we should be curious about the answers.

OUT   145

1 Marie Le Conte, "Death Threats, Rape Threats and Relentless Abuse: The Scandal Rocking French Media," *New Statesman*, February 13, 2019, https://www.newstatesman.com/politics/2019/02/death-threats-rape-threats-and-relentless-abuse-scandal-rocking-french-media, accessed December 20, 2021.

2 Virginia Woolf, *Three Guineas* (London: Penguin, 1977), p. 118.

3 Ibid., pp. 123–25.

4 Ibid., p. 68.

5 Ibid., p. 72.

6 Ibid., pp. 76, 86.

7 Ibid., p. 96.

8 Katherine Angel, *Tomorrow Sex Will Be Good Again: Women and Desire in the Age of Consent* (London: Verso, 2021).

9 Holly Yan, Eliott C. McLaughlin, and Dana Ford, "Bill Cosby Admitted to Getting Quaaludes to Give to Women," CNN, July 7, 2015, https://edition.cnn.com/2015/07/07/us/bill-cosby-quaaludes-sexual-assault-allegations/index.html, accessed December 20, 2021.

10 Charles W. Mills, *The Racial Contract* (Ithaca, NY: Cornell University Press, 1997), p. 18.

11 Shannon Sullivan and Nancy Tuana, introduction to *Race and Epistemologies of Ignorance*, eds. Shannon Sullivan and Nancy Tuana (Albany: State University of New York Press, 2007), pp. 1–10, here p. 1.

12 Robert Booth, "George Galloway Wades into Julian Assange Row—And Creates a Storm," *The Guardian*, August 20, 2012, https://www.theguardian.com/media/2012/aug/20/george-galloway-julian-assange-rape, accessed December 20, 2021.

13 *Girls*, season 1, episode 3, "All Adventurous Women Do," written and directed by Lena Dunham, aired April 29, 2012, on HBO.

14 Brooke Magnanti, *The Sex Myth: Why Everything We're Told Is Wrong* (London: Weidenfeld & Nicolson, 2013), p. 11, emphasis added.

15 *Crazy, Stupid, Love*, directed by Glenn Ficarra and John Requa, written by Dan Fogelman, featuring Steve Carell, Ryan Gosling, Julianne Moore, and Emma Stone (Burbank, CA: Warner Bros. Pictures, 2011).

16 Rebecca Traister, "Why Sex That's Consensual Can Still Be Bad. And Why We're Not Talking About It," *The Cut*, October 20, 2015, https://www.thecut.com/2015/10/why-consensual-sex-can-still-be-bad.html, accessed December 20, 2021; Christina Tesoro, "Not So Bad: On Consent, Non-Consent, and Trauma," *The Toast*, November 9, 2015, https://the-toast.net/2015/11/09/consent-non-consent-trauma/, accessed December 20, 2021; Melissa Febos, "I Spent My Life Consenting to Touch I Didn't Want," *New York Times Magazine*, March 31, 2021, https://www.nytimes.com/2021/03/31/magazine/consent.html, accessed December 20, 2021.

146 THE　WAY

The Way Out: Letter to New Activists

Paul B. Preciado

 THE

WAY

Friends, I am filled with joy. Not because things are going well, as you might imagine. But because we have the collective capacity to become aware of what is happening and, for the first time in history, to share this experience on a global scale: to exchange social technologies, knowledge, perceptions, affects, and to make practices and knowledges that were previously subaltern shared by all.

Awareness is neither an intellectual process nor a simple strategic management of forms of struggle. Becoming aware implies, as Édouard Glissant taught us, *trembling*:[1] feeling that we are part of the problem we want to solve. And, therefore, to understand that there will be no possible change that does not imply a mutation of our own processes of political subjectivation, of our modes of production, of consumption, of reproduction, of nomination, of relation, of our ways of representing, of desiring, of loving. To become aware is to realize that our own living and desiring body is the only social technology able to operate the change.

Some will say that there is no reason to be optimistic. There is not a single social space in which the signs of advancing technologies of death are not already felt as an imminent threat to all living things. We have destroyed more of the ecosystem in the last two centuries than in two million years, during the entire history of the Quaternary. What we have so far called neoliberalism must be redefined as necro-capitalism: the specialization of the technologies of sex-racial capitalism in the transformation of life, of all life, into *dead capital,* reproductive labor, and *dead pleasure.* We have turned the biosphere and all that inhabits it into a source of energy that we seek to extract and accumulate. We have stripped the earth, each and every body of every organ, and extracted every fluid. Racialization and hierarchical sexualization of the human species, mining, clearing of forests, destruction of the marine ecosystem, industrialization of animal and human reproduction, development of war industries. But can we afford the luxury of pessimism? Christian Thomas, a specialist in fossil fuels, states, when talking about contemporary energy management, that "we don't have a problem of rare materials, we have a problem of grey matter."[2] But we don't even have a gray matter problem—the specialized neuronal functions of our species are sufficient and even excessive—we have a problem of organization of sensitivity, of structure of desire. We have a problem of addiction to the consumption of *dead capital* and *dead pleasure.*

If, in the midst of this shit, I am invaded if not by optimism then at least by enthusiasm, it is because I saw you coming out of the Place Clichy metro by the hundreds, coming from all the streets, from the north and the south, from the suburbs and from the center of Paris, walking alone, in groups, arriving on a scooter or on foot, and gathering in the park like a flock of birds landing in unison. I saw you march fearlessly toward the courthouse to shout together, in a thousand languages, the name of Adama Traoré. I heard you shout, from across the Atlantic, the names of George Floyd, Jamal Sutherland, Patrick Warren, Kevin Lavira Desir, Erik Mejia, Randy Miller. I saw you write the names of Patsy Andrea Delgado, Alexa Negrón Luciano, Serena Angelique Velázquez, Layla Pelaez Sánchez, Yampi Méndez Arocho, Penélope Díaz Ramírez, Michelle Michellyn Ramos Vargas, Selena Reyes-Hernandez, Valera, Ebeng Mayor … on the walls. I have seen you take to the streets in Valaparaíso and Santiago de Chile, in Istanbul's Taksim Square, on the Cerro de Bolivia, in Los Angeles and San Francisco, in Madrid's Puerta del Sol and in front of Ayotzinapa's teacher-training college.

WAY

I have walked beside you.

And I am no longer afraid of what might happen.

You are young, almost children, and you dare to look in the face of the police forces surrounding you. Don't they feel awkward to be dressed for war in front of you, a crowd of unarmed and almost naked kids? I refer to you with the nonbinary gender not because among you there are no bodies that have been assigned the male or female gender at birth and do not identify as nonbinary. I do it to give you back the nonbinarity that you deserve. The one that is due to you and that was stolen from you. And to emphasize that it is the body in rebellion against gender-racial epistemology that is now standing up to the past. For years I have addressed you first as a lesbian, then as a trans persona, as a nonbinary gendered body, as a migrant, as a foreigner. Now I want to speak to you as a living being, not as an organism that is the object of a biological or medical discourse, nor as a force of reproduction or production. But as a desiring power, as a sensitive body that goes beyond the binary taxonomies of modernity. And I address you for all that you are, situated in the dense network of economic, racial, sexual, bodily powers. With your own history of oppression and survival. You have been racialized, sexualized, you are women, queer, trans, nonbinary, racialized, migrant, sick, crip … and anyone who doesn't feel represented in this *somatopolitical Lumpenproletariat,* in this universal minority, need only explain why, need only say if there is something else they want to claim, and if not, they should just join you.

They say, as June Jordan wrote, that you are the wrong age, that you have the wrong skin, the wrong sex, the wrong hair, the wrong gender, the wrong desire, the wrong dream, the wrong shoes, the wrong pronouns, the wrong prosthetics, the wrong codes, the wrong tastes, the wrong interests,

the wrong relationships, the wrong memory, the
wrong gestures, the wrong intentions, the wrong
readings, that you are on the wrong ground, on the
wrong continent. *But you are not wrong. Wrong is not
your name.*[3] Until now, you have been taught to be
ashamed of your differences that they have called
"dysphoria." But your history of oppression is your
diamond; you must study it and know it, make it
a collective archive for change and survival. Your
dysphoria is your resistance to the norm, in it lies the
power to transform the present. Only the knowledge
that emerges from this trauma and this violence,
from this shame and this pain, from this inadequacy
and this abnormality can save us.

The dimension of the sex-racial capitalist destruction of life requires a change in the understanding of
politics, a deepening of the levels of struggle, a move
away from the segmented identity languages that
separate and even oppose anti-capitalist, ecological,
anti-racist, anti-patriarchal, feminist, queer, and trans
struggles to imagine the whole process of systemic
mutation (linguistic, cognitive, libidinal, energetic,
institutional, relational . . .). There will be no step
toward a new epistemic regime without a radical
transformation of the hierarchical taxonomy of living
bodies and of their differential access to planetary
energy. This *transitional revolution* is also the one
where the alliance of anti-racist and transfeminist
struggles will allow the definition of a new framework of intelligibility for living bodies.

I have seen you and I know now that you are more
radical and intelligent, more beautiful and more
hybrid than we have ever been. I say "beautiful," but
it's not the heteronormative, colonial standards of
beauty we grew up with: the thin white body, the
blonde hair, the light eyes. Symmetrical, smiling,
valid. It is instead a beauty that you invent by
claiming other lives and other bodies, other desires,

and other words. It is the beauty of the fat body, of the
wheelchair, of the Afro hair, of the sick body, of the
feminine muscles and the masculine curves, of the
hoarse or soft voice, but above all the beauty of the
obstinacy and the memory, of the attention and the
tenderness that you have for each other. I am sur-
prised that you are capable of such kindness in the
midst of this war. If such tenderness is possible, then
perhaps it is possible to make this paradigm shift.

I have seen you and I can only salute your courage,
your decisiveness, your precision of words, your
strategic intelligence, your love, your generosity, the
way you overcame the naturalizing identity politics
of the end of the last century, the thirst with which
you distanced yourselves from the neoliberal ideal
of success to join the network of monsters and the
mycelium, the fungal, plant, animal, and mineral
cooperation. You are not victims. You are survivors.
You have survived the abuse, the rape, the desire
of the colonial fathers to destroy their children, but
above all, you have for the first time found words to
name this pain, and with these words, with your pain
not raw, but transformed, with your pain not named
with its pathologizing categories, but with your own
words, you have also discovered a new strength, a
new desire that can no longer be reduced to either
Freud's patriarchal prophecies or Marx's virile class
struggle in the name of progress.

And, looking at you, I feel like moving away from
the generation that was mine, to join yours.

That's why I want to get closer to you and leave
the world I knew, because if we are where we are,
it is because of our mistakes. I am talking about my
generation and my parents' generation. It is we and
your parents who preferred to forget that our free
market was based on slavery and oppression, that
our democracies were built on the crimes of colonization and genocide. We preferred to forget that

we defeated Nazism by dropping two atomic bombs.
That our wealth was built on exploitation, plunder,
and destruction. We preferred to trivialize torture
and institutionalize violence, to affirm the difference
between national and foreign, in order to consolidate
our economic and racial privileges. We accepted the
heterosexual and monogamous family as the best
(and almost the only) institution of affection and
normal filiation, and we fought for access to it. We
believed that our freedom would come from access
as consumers to the marketplace, as citizens to the
nation, and as husbands and fathers to the family.

We are the ones who have consented to everything
that has happened: we have abused you, we have
preferred to forget the grievances of colonization and
slavery, we have exchanged desire for consumption,
we have given up the power of feminist emancipation
in exchange for the presence of a few white, heterosexual women in government positions, we have
abandoned revolution to promote economic growth,
we have exchanged sexual rebellion for the normal-
ization of homosexuals and their integration into the
dominant heterosexual culture, we have considered
it relevant to abandon the demand for restitution and
decolonization in exchange for "tolerance" and the
integration of "others" into European culture.

Even the left said that the class struggles had to
come first, that sexual and racial struggles would
come later—but what came later, in a big way, was not
revolution, but neoliberalism. It was the left that saw
feminist, queer, and trans struggles as insufficiently
manly and patriotic, that preferred to label them "the
race question," as the "communitarist danger." It was
my generation that preferred to spend its days and
nights fighting for the right to gay marriage rather
than for the acquisition of equal and just citizenship
rights for all living bodies on the planet, wherever
they come from and wherever they are.

WA

You have not participated in it: you have already arrived in a world that has made normalizing, racist, and fascist decisions, that has signed a contract with the financial devil. Your addiction to consumption and communication—which is just another form of consumption, this time semiotic—your desire to be represented and accepted by the majority, has been instilled in you from the cradle. We gave you blood and oil to drink, plastic, fear, and electricity to eat. We have injected the heroin of capital into your veins. And now it's up to you to do the only thing you can do if you want to survive: detox. Change your body and your cognitive regime, desire differently, love what we have taught you to hate.

This is why I feel, seeing you walking toward the court, taking over the squares, filling the walls with graffiti ... that I must leave my generation to join yours.

Your revolutionary heritage comes not from your genetic parents, but from an underground and lateral transmission of affects and knowledge, a cultural and bastard smuggling that defies clans, genes, borders, and names. I watch you speak quietly in front of a crowd and I know that you are the children of Sojourner Truth and Angela Davis, that you are maroons who escaped slavery; you have the wisdom of that journey, you know the way. You are the followers of Emma Goldman and Voltairine de Cleyre. You prefer cooperation to individual achievement. You are the impossible offspring that Malcolm X and Martin Luther King Jr. would have conceived if they had been able to love each other carnally. You have made possible the convergence of civil disobedience and the affirmation of the pride of Black culture, the impossible progeny that Michel Foucault would have had with Franz Fanon if the French professor had not been in the closet and exoticized racialized bodies and if the Algerian activist had not been

so macho and homophobic. Maybe that's why you
go so much further than them, why you invent
another movement and another world. You are the
superchords. You are the equals of Jean Genet and
James Baldwin. It is your imagination that guides
you beyond your memory. You are the companions
of Annie Sprinkle and Beth Stephens, of Virginie
Despentes and Binyavanga Wainaina, because you no
longer have to hide the fact that you have been raped,
because you no longer have to apologize for your
lesbianism, for your excess of sexual desire, because
you know that this desire is also what nourishes the
transformation to come.

I listen to you talk about institutional violence and
decolonization and I know that you are my masters.
And that is why I choose you as my only ancestors,
as both my legacy and my inheritance, as my only
genealogy and my only future. I tell you all this
because I was a trans child, a cursed body of fascism.
I was born in a Spain still under the yoke of Franco,
where one lived in terror of being denounced and
where being poor, being Black, being an unmarried
mother, being queer, transvestite, crazy, disabled . . .
meant being a dissident of the system and finally
being the object of its violence. It was a Spain, a
Mediterranean country inhabited by brown-skinned
people, composed of converted Muslims and Jews,
which, denying this reality, nevertheless boasted
of being the cradle of Christianity, of having been a
white colonizing empire. But in the many peoples
that make up Spain, we have never been white, in any
case neither more nor less white than the Moroccans
or the French, because whiteness is not a "fact"; it is,
as Achille Mbembe teaches us, not a "melanin principle."[4] It does not exist empirically: it is a technology
of government and violence that produces social and
political vulnerability.[5] And now, when I hear you
shouting the name of those murdered by the police,

when I see you taking to the streets to demand justice
for the victims of institutional racism, institutional
transcide, rape, or femicide, I feel that I want to leave
this normative whiteness that has been imposed
on me as a requirement, I want to leave the "white
solipsism"[6] that has been given to me as a privilege
and as a norm, as a sovereignty, and as an order, and
I want to be your child, because I have so much to
unlearn from my colonial ancestors and so much to
learn from you.

That's why I want to become a child again and
make the revolution with you now, take off the white
skin of privilege and wear the skin of childhood once
and for all, because my childhood, my name, and my
history have been stolen from me and because I don't
want a handful of bodies who think they're normal
and white to steal anyone's childhood, name, and
history again.

I can't offer much useful advice for a time of change
like yours. It is not you who need my advice. It's me
who needs yours. Except to tell you—since I am
a mutant and all the happiness I have known has
come from that mutation—to embrace the mutation
intensely instead of worrying about reforming
existing institutions. We have already wasted too
much time integrating ourselves into the dominant
sex-racial capitalist binary and heteropatriarchal
culture, dealing with its languages, negotiating small
margins of maneuver.

Don't expect messiahs or heroes: on the contrary,
messiahs and heroes have been our fundamental
historical problems. Don't expect anything from
institutions either: they are dead, or rather, they
are the vampire organs of the sex-racial apparatus
against which we must fight. Don't expect anything
from the family as such. It is not as fathers or
children, as mothers or siblings that you can take
care of each other, because these relationships are

OUT   159

already mediated by networks of power, ownership, exploitation, and inheritance. It is from those with whom you do not know how to relate, from those who escape normative institutional protocols, that transformation can come. Learn from all that is not human and its methods of energy extraction and distribution. This does not mean abandoning your parents and sisters, but establishing the same relationship with them that you establish with trees, mushrooms, birds, bees, and vice versa; only then can you invent a new bond. Treat your parents and sisters as trees and bees, and the bees and trees as if they were your parents and sisters.

Don't waste your time organizing e-judgments of representatives of the old sex-racial regime either. J. K. Rowling's transphobia is not worth the expenditure of mutant energy. Instead, focus on designing mutation, repairing what has been destroyed, and inventing new practices and forms of relationships, while the Rowlings of the Capitalocene are busy explaining to you that you are male or female based on whether or not you bleed from your genital orifices. You are no longer what the Rowlings of all sides are trying to designate. You are all the orifices of the world. You are the universal anus and vagina. You are the crevices of the poles. You are the hole in the ozone layer. And none of this needs to be proved or defended. It just is. And not only do you know it, but you have decided to act. That is why, my friends, I am filled with joy.

1 Édouard Glissant, *Philosophie de la relation* (Paris: Gallimard, 2009), pp. 54–56.

2 Christian Thomas, "Dépendance aux métaux stratégiques," Conseil économique, social et environnemental, January 22, 2019, https://www.lecese.fr/content/la-dependance-aux-metaux-strategiques-quelles-solutions-pour-leconomie, accessed January 10, 2022.

3 Variation on June Jordan, "Poem about My Rights," in *Directed by Desire: The Collected Poems of June Jordan* (Port Townsend, WA: Copper Canyon, 2005).

4 Achille Mbembe, *Critique of Black Reason* (Durham, NC: Duke University Press, 2017), pp. 42–43.

5 Judith Butler, Zeynep Gambetti, and Leticia Sabsay, introduction to *Vulnerability in Resistance* ed. Judith Butler, Zeynep Gambetti, and Leticia Sabsay (Durham, NC: Duke University Press, 2016), pp. 1–11, here p. 5.

6 Adrienne Rich, a feminist thinker who abdicated her own whiteness through love, friendship, and political work with Michelle Cliff and Audre Lorde, defines "white solipsism" as that position of power that exhorts us to speak, imagine, and think as if "white" experience described the totality of the world. Adrienne Rich, "'Disloyal to Civilization': Feminism, Racism, and Gynephobia," in *On Lies, Secrets, and Silence: Selected Prose 1966–1978* (New York: W. W. Norton, 1979), pp. 275–310, here p. 299.

Ways
Out of the
White Cube
and the
Black Box

Dorothea
von
Hantelmann

164 THE WAY

The neo-avant-gardes of the 1960s and 1970s, especially in their event-oriented branches, were driven by an oppositional stance to the conventions of visual art and theater. They were carried by the utopian belief that it is possible to create something that exists outside of these conventions, outside of the market and the museums, but also outside the framework of theater.

The phenomenon we witness today is very different. In recent years, the art world has developed a keen interest in new formats that combine the modalities of exhibiting and performing. In the process, the borders between the visual and the performing arts are dissolving: exhibitions turn into dramaturgically designed time spaces in which a sequence of events unfold. Hybrids between exhibition and event emerge, incorporating the performative nature of theater or specific elements such as temporal sequence and integration into the exhibition.

Theater today functions as a kind of toolbox for the visual arts; it provides techniques that artists from other fields use. At the same time, as art museums are being redesigned and reoriented, there is a strong reevaluation of live performances. Concerts, DJ sets, lectures, or workshops, which previously belonged to the accompanying program and had a rather peripheral status, are now advancing to become an integral part of art exhibitions, making them more and more like programmed festivals. Performed art reached the heart of museums at the latest in early 2010, when in New York the Guggenheim Museum opened an exhibition by Tino Sehgal and a short time later MoMA opened an exhibition by Marina Abramović.[1]

One consequence of this development is the increased interest in dance: contemporary choreographers (such as Meg Stuart, Boris Charmatz, or

Xavier Le Roy) are invited to present their work in museums, while in the performing arts—in dance and theater—interest in the visual arts is growing. Firstly, this field still promises a different kind of relevance or legitimacy on a discursive level that is attractive to artists from other fields. Secondly, the format of the exhibition allows for what the theater cannot produce on its own: individualized and flexibilized forms of experience. Thus, in the theater, too, sporadic experiments with addressing visitors in an individual and isolated manner are made, or work is done on new flexibilized performance formats that also include aspects of installations.[2]

Curators and institutions are also searching for new formats, often in the context of festivals that programmatically open up to other art forms and discourses and are at the same time more flexible in terms of formats than theaters and museums.[3] For about a decade now, an increasing number of art institutions have been trying to integrate live art into the exhibition space in different ways.[4] Time will tell whether hierarchies will actually begin to shift and whether the prioritization of visual art will slowly come to an end.

~~Ritualistic Topologies: Exhibition and Performance~~

One lesson to be learned from the avant-gardes is that conventions are powerful. For many avant-garde practices the reintegration into the museum meant a return to the very conventions that they had originally rejected. If one wants to operate within cultural formats, it is helpful to understand their historical (and present) meaning and function.

Art institutions—museums, exhibitions, theaters, concert halls, festivals—have never been merely containers for artworks. They historically drew and still draw their symbolic power and social legitimacy

from the fact that they celebrate, embody, and enact
the foundational categories and values of a society.
They have an impact on the conduct and behavior
of people, shaping it according to the core concepts
and values of the societies in which they exist.[5] At
the same time, the power of these venues is derived
not only—and perhaps not even primarily—from
the art they present. The social and political power
of museums and theaters comes from the format as
a whole. By format, I mean the spatial arrangement
between performers and spectators, or artworks and
viewers, that constitutes the spatial-discursive space
for what is shown. Independently of what is actually
performed in a theater or exhibited in a museum,
irrespective of what transpires in terms of media
or genre, the manner in which this relationship is
organized itself assumes significance by deploying
very particular values and formats. And because
theaters and museums are different cultural formats,
the values and worldviews attributed to and brought
into effect by them are respectively different.

From the perspective of ritual theory, theaters and
museums can be seen as specific forms of gatherings, as rituals. Every society generates its rituals of
gathering, and the structure of these rituals tells us
something about the structure of these societies.
For the Greek city state, for example, the theater
was a highly significant place of gathering, just as
the cathedral was in medieval society. Despite their
obvious differences, the theater and the church share
similarities in their structure: there is one that speaks
to the many, one sender and many receivers—a
structure that corresponds to the hierarchical social
structure of premodern societies.

For an emerging democratic mass society, this
modality couldn't work any longer. It's not possible
to gather a nation of ten million all in one place
and it doesn't correspond to the self-understanding

of a modern individualized society. The modern
nation needed new forms of gatherings: a new
ritual, so to speak. This is where the museum
comes in. The "national gallery" is a place where
the nation can gather but not all at the same time.
The key invention, if you like, was the introduction
of opening hours, because they enable a shift from
the modality of the appointment on which theater is
based (where all come together in a fixed time frame)
to more individualized, liberalized forms of usage
and gathering. Within the relatively loose temporal
frame of the museum's opening hours, everyone can
come and go as they like, decide themselves where
to go, what to focus their attention on. There is no
collective direction of attention, no common action
to be taken.

In its focus on the individual and on individualized and flexibilized forms of usage, the museum is a
distinctly modern cultural format that corresponds
to an equally modern, liberal, and individualized
sensitivity. Seen in this light, the national gallery
is not only a place where the cultural wealth of a
nation is presented, but it is also a place where the
modern nation gathers in its specifically modern
structure—that is, not as a collective body but as
a gathering of individuals. Today, many museums
and exhibitions receive thousands of visitors per
day, but every individual nevertheless participates
in his or her own way. To create a format that
(at least according to its own claims) is open to
all but not the same for everybody—embracing
mass accessibility and individualization, two
essential building blocks of modern mass democracies—can be seen, when viewed historically,
as an essential achievement of the museum. And
because it provides a clear reflection of how we
understand modern democracies, the museum
still constitutes a core ritual of these societies.

WAY

In this conceptual framework, the theater and the museum—or, in more general terms, the stage and the exhibition format—can be regarded as two different ritualistic topologies. They differ in character, they differ in what they impart to society, and they differ in terms of their function and significance within the huge transformational process that generated modern societies. The history of theater, based on the modality of the appointment, is one of forming and organizing collectives. The particular strength of this appointment modality lies in the creation of a collective body as well as its organization.

Over the centuries, theater cultivated techniques for bundling the heterogeneous energies of its many spectators and for unfolding an affective power over them that at times is also inverted. But as a format, it does not create a liberal space in the modern sense. One enters the theater as an audience, as a collective body, and, upon exiting, one must quite literally press oneself out of this collective body again. The power of the exhibition format lies precisely in that it does not require participants to commit to a shared time frame, nor to certain spelled-out statements. Rather, it creates a space in which pluralism is cultivated (every collection, every exhibition, is a polyphony of varied subjectivities) along with a "solidarity without consensus."[6] The trade-off for this openness is a format that is energetically "cooler" and, precisely because of its liberal character, relatively affectless.

Historically, almost all cultural formats were based on the modality of the appointment, in which the one addresses the many. It took centuries to generate a cultural setting that would be based on the more modern, individualized, and liberal modality in which the many speak to each other. Just as the format of the appointment is tied to certain forms of incorporation—for example, by creating a period of time shared by all spectators for the duration of

the performance or the ritual—the opening-hours
format operates by the dissolution of such forms of
incorporation. Historically, this was driven by an
emancipatory impetus; it was about cultivating the
disengagement from the social ties and structures of
feudal and aristocratic societies.

If we look at 19th- and 20th-century museum
spaces, we can trace the process of individualization
and thus the decisive social dynamic of modern
societies based on the increasing distance between
the exhibited objects: from the crowded presen-
tation in 19th-century museums, with no focus on
individual objects, to the open and rather spare
exhibition spaces of the 20th century, where the
crowded-togetherness of artifacts and viewers has
given way to spaces that are almost entirely cleared.
The singled-out individual encounters a material
object that is equally singled-out. It is taken out of its
preexisting networks. The exhibited artwork is an
ex-*hibited* artwork. It is extracted from its original
context in order to be shown and experienced as an
artwork. Historically, this context might have been
the altar of a church, from which the painting has
been removed, or the decorative system of a royal
court, of which the artwork formed part before it was
included into the museum collection. The display of
the artwork is preceded by an act of separation.

This cultivation of disengagement, of separation
(of nature from culture, the individual from other
individuals, visuality from other senses and so on),
which plays out in the museum on so many levels,
is closely linked to a modern, secular concept of
society, which also implies a specific notion of time.
Time in museums is reduced to the evolutionary
concept of historical epochs. The museum advanced
to become something like a new ritual for modern
societies precisely because it overcame theater's
model of a collective audience, in which everyone is

 WA

subject to the same time frame. And again, it is this flexibility that makes the exhibition a ritual that is aligned with a modern, individualized sensitivity. But what allows for this flexibility is the fact that the artwork doesn't have an explicit time of its own. It doesn't demand a specific time; it doesn't need to be synchronized with the time of the viewer. In contrast to theater and cinema, there is no requirement for a specific organization of time to which the individual must succumb. In short: the atemporal artwork, that artwork that does not unfold in time, is structurally linked to the exhibition as a flexible, individualized modern ritual.

Limitations of the Existing Formats

In general terms, two primary modalities of ritual gathering have found their forms of cultivation and institutionalization in what used to be called modern Western societies: collective gatherings and individual gatherings. Collective gatherings that are based on the modality of the appointment: there is a group of people, a collective, that gathers at the same place and time in order to attend to the shared experience of listening and/or seeing. And individualized gatherings that are based on the modality of opening hours: people gather at certain locations to pursue activities that are accessible to everyone but that do not necessarily need to be carried out or experienced in a group (which is why one could object that, strictly speaking, one is not dealing here with gatherings).

Both modalities have institutionalized themselves in the arts. In fact, contemporary cultural institutions are based on either the collective or the individualized modality. The collective gathering, tied to the topology of the room divided between stage and spectator, incorporates events such as theater and dance performances, lectures, and concerts. The

individualized format, which produces individualized and flexible forms of experience, is put into
practice in exhibitions and museums. The underlying thesis of this essay, however, is that neither
modality—collective nor individualized—can meet
the requirements of today's forms of social coexistence. Broadly speaking, I argue that the modality
of the appointment, though capable of generating
a collective body with a certain energetic intensity,
is too rigid in the concept of the collective that it
enacts. At the same time, the modality of opening
hours, as cultivated by museums and exhibitions, is
more liberal and flexible, but lacks a sense of social
cohesion, which is a quality that we yearn for in these
individualized, flexible times.

The concepts of theater and exhibition are based
on conditions that in the past decades have changed
more fundamentally than the formats themselves
did. To a certain extent, one might say that they
have both fallen out of their time: theater finds its
dominant form—especially in the German-speaking
context—as a place of assembly for urban society.
A prefabricated idea of collectivity is inherent in it;
it is set in stone, as it were, in the building, and thus
difficult to break apart and replace with more flexible
and fluid forms of address and assembly.

The museum, on the other hand, emerges as a
temple of the productivist, materialist society, which
is extremely focused on things, and which needs
places to rehearse the refined reflection on objects
or processes of self-awareness in relation to the
object. In today's society, this focus on the object is
no longer so central. The valences have changed.
Social context and human relations become more
important. A society that is no longer so dead set
on things, in which objects no longer have this
central position, also turns to forms of interaction
in its rituals. In this context, the exhibition format

increasingly appears to be too static, too antisocial, and too focused on the object.

Toward a New Ritual Format

How to create a format that temporarily brings people together in nonrigid ways, that introduces moments of connectivity without falling back on inherited and calcified conceptions of the collective? What would a ritual space look like that establishes connectivity, and yet remains in tune with a contemporary, individualized, and flexibilized sensibility? These are central questions inscribed in the current artistic and curatorial search for new formats. They are supported and promoted by a social dimension negotiated in a theoretical as well as practical manner: How can highly individualized, fragmented, heterogeneous societies produce moments and experiences of connectivity? How can bonds, or forms of attachment, be established without giving up flexibility and individualization? How can social bonds be lived that are sustainable without being rigid?

We are moving toward the idea of a new ritual, which—considered speculatively—would have to absorb both the changes and the challenges of the 21st century. Three criteria seem central to me: First, the new ritual should be able to connect the individual with the collective. There have been approaches in the visual arts since the 1990s that go in this direction. A phenomenon that seems particularly interesting in this context is the emergence of the time-based exhibition: an exhibition that de facto changes in time.[7] I see these time-based exhibitions that I would like to call "individualized spaces for events" as part of the emergence of a new ritual format that is more suited to the necessities and values of the 21st century. The "individualized space for events" is essentially a hybrid between

exhibition and event space. In its temporal mode
and as a dramaturgical composition in time, it is
on the one hand close to a theatrical live event.
Things happen there in time, so there is a structural
proximity to a theater performance that takes place
in time. Objects are not only inserted in space but
also in time, making time the explicit structuring
element of the exhibition—thereby creating its own
time into which the viewer is drawn. It's a way of
fusing artworks and visitors into a shared time span
and creating a different attention span or modality
of attention. Forms of connectivity need time: they
emerge in time, which is why time becomes such
an important factor in these exhibitions. Yet, in
their mode of address, these spaces stay attuned
to the liberal and individualized principle of the
exhibition. They keep the liberal framework of the
opening hours; visitors are grouped, but they are
grouped in temporary clusters rather than in a fixed
collective. And the collectivity that is generated is
relatively loose and liberal. These spaces experi-
ment with new modes of addressing that are on the
one hand more oriented toward the creation of ties
or connectivities than the traditional exhibition
format was able to generate. On the other hand, they
stay attuned to a contemporary individualized and
flexibilized sensitivity.

The second criterion of the new ritual space would
be its grounding in an ontology based not on the
modern imperative of separation and autonomy but
on modalities of connectedness and permeability.
The question that increasingly concerns us is
how the dualisms on which the modern order is
based—society and nature, spirit and matter, theory
and practice—can be overcome; how everything
that has been separated—nature from culture,
product from process, the individual from social
ties, rationality from other modalities of knowledge

WA

and consciousness, and the like—can be connected. Traditionally, museums and theaters are spaces that block the outside world. The modern belief system of a strict separation of nature and culture manifests itself in them. More than anything, the 20th-century white cube is a flexible, disconnected kind of Cartesian space, cleared and freed of all real-world influences where all natural processes and vibrations—temperature, light, acoustics—are regulated. A new ritual space, in contrast, would be characterized by a porosity toward its outside environment. I have elsewhere sketched out the idea of a "situated artwork,"[8] which is integrated into a habitat, an ecosystem, into living processes. The question would be how exhibitions as such could also be situated in such a way, visibly and invisibly connected to the place in which they exist. Situatedness, understood in this way, above all means recognizing that any categorical separation is a fiction, a construction.

Finally, the third criterion for a new ritual that paves the way out of the white cube and the black box would be a more active conception of the partaker, the beholder. While theaters and museums conceptualize the partaker primarily as a recipient, as a passive viewer or spectator, my hypothesis is that a 21st-century ritual will eventually—like in traditional rituals and along with contemporary knowledge societies and creative societies—conceptualize the partaker as a participant who can freely choose to be (or not be) active and thus can both actively and passively contribute to the outcome of the ritual. What I see as the way out of the white cube and black box is a new ritual, which is individualized but social, which is porous and interconnected and allows both for activity and passivity on the side of its partaking citizens.

OUT 175

1   *Tino Sehgal*, Solomon R. Guggenheim Museum, New York, January 29–March 10, 2010; *Marina Abramović: The Artist Is Present*, MoMA, New York, March 14–May 31, 2010.

2   As examples, one could list various projects by Gob Squad and Stefan Kaegi / Rimini Protokoll, but also early experiments such as Felix Ruckert's *Hautnah* (1995) at Berlin's Dock 11.

3   In 2007, for example, the project *Il Tempo del Postino* was curated by Hans Ulrich Obrist and Philippe Parreno for the Manchester International Festival, a project for which mainly visual artists were invited to present short live sequences on the stage of a theater. This was followed in 2011 by the live exhibition *11 Rooms*, also curated for the Manchester International Festival by Hans Ulrich Obrist and Klaus Biesenbach.

4   The forerunner was the Tate Modern with its Tanks, opened in 2012 and expanded in 2016, which are programmed similarly to a festival and are both exhibition and performance venues—that is, they show live performances as well as film or video installations. In 2019, New York's MoMA followed suit with a new performance art space and a series of performances curated specifically for this "studio."

5   The art historian Carol Duncan, for instance, describes the museum as a "civilizing ritual" for citizens in modern democracies, while sociologist Tony Bennett speaks of them as "civic laboratories," that is, training grounds for civilized and civilizing behavior. Carol Duncan, *Civilizing Rituals: Inside Public Art Museums* (London: Routledge, 1995); Tony Bennett, *The Birth of the Museum: History, Theory, Politics* (London: Routledge, 1995), p. 47.

6   See David Kertzer, *Ritual, Politics, and Power* (New Haven: Yale University Press, 1989).

7   My own work on this theme draws on artists such as Pierre Huyghe, Philippe Parreno, Anri Sala, Tino Sehgal, and Dominique Gonzalez-Foerster, who have been working on the temporalization of the exhibition since the early 2000s. Again, many other approaches have been developed over the past decade, both on an artistic and a curatorial level.

8   Dorothea von Hantelmann, "Situated Cosmo-Technologies: Pierre Huyghe's *Untilled* and *After ALife Ahead*," in *Pierre Huyghe: Werke / Works 2009–2019*, ed. Rebecca Lewin and Natalia Grabowska (London: Koenig, 2019), pp. 10–25.

The Way Out, Out, Out

Thomas Hirschhorn

 THE WAY

We might have thought, following the Coronavirus policies of masks, distancing, lockdowns, inoculations, that these responses would be the way out, and that with time, all would pass. But we didn't see the bigger picture, because the change was very slow, beyond our scope of recognition. We didn't see all the scars being carved into our social body. We didn't measure how our relations and interactions were changing. Now, after almost two years, we look at each other in awe. Did she get it? Did he get it? Will he ask? Should I ask her? What do we think? What did we experience during all that time—what did we live for?

The negation of the negative does not necessarily produce the positive. And here, the negative and the positive seem to have switched places in order to perform an exclusion of people instead of the virus—or rather an exclusion of the non-vaccinated. However, from the beginning, my work has been based on non-exclusivity. To work for and include a "Non-Exclusive Audience" fulfills one of my most important missions. The "Non-Exclusive Audience" is indubitably the hard core of my projects. To address the "Non-Exclusive Audience" under all circumstances, to fight any and all "elitism," to break down the tendency of self-enclosure and oppose the temptation of isolation or self-isolation has always been my mission. My work has always aimed at the "impossible," which means creating an encounter, a real encounter, and this "impossible" can only be accomplished on the basis of total inclusivity. I have written about it and I have lived it throughout my works in public space based on the principle of "Presence and Production." Art is an absolute, inclusive movement. Art must include the "Non-Exclusive Audience," the Other, the neighbor, the stranger, the person on the margin, the uninterested. Art can never act in exclusion—for any reason, Art can never act in resentment or negativity. Art is always and in all circumstances against all kinds of discrimination. Art is openness to the presence of the Other, the presence of everybody, not only of those who can present whatever passport, whatever legitimacy or kind of code. Therefore, I can't accept any exclusion due to the differentiation between vaccinated, cured, or non-vaccinated. As an artist who has worked and wants to work for and with a "Non-Exclusive Audience," it's just not possible; there's no way I can accept this kind of segregation within my work.

Art institutions today have been humiliated by being qualified as "non-essential"—and with them everybody who loves and believes in Art. Less so for the artist, since every artist knows his or her non-essentiality, and since each artwork is an attempt to prove the necessity of its existence as such. We know that Art—all Art of all times and all places—crosses borders. That Art—all Art of all times and all places—never builds walls, never establishes borders, or imagines separations. Not the institutions. They're now trying to regain their essentiality—but only for one group of people. They gave up on their inclusivity without protest, following every sanitary instruction without any complaint or protest—or at least, it was long forgotten—only concerned with filling up their spaces and proving their essentiality again. On their way out they forgot what the mission of a museum and art institution is. In their panic, they confronted their death—not the individual death nor the death of the social body, but the death of the cultural institution—and were willing to accept every atrocity, every exclusion, every split.

Therefore, the way out is—again, again, and again— the way out of art institutions. The Coronavirus crisis has pointed this out in the extreme—asking once again: "What is your position? What do you want? What is your mission? What kind of relation are you

                    WAY

creating toward the world? What kind of critique are you establishing within your work?" Those are the questions that we need to confront and to which we—artists—need to give a response in our work.

I will now draw three necessary "Way-Outs": "The Way Out of … the COVID-19 Response," "The Way Out … into Public Space," and "The Way Out of … Obsolete Institutional and Museum Practices into 'The Museum of The Future.'"

~~The Way Out of … the COVID-19 Response~~

The way out of the COVID-19 crisis and its response is urgent. We must get out now, out, out, out! We must see this way out as an urgent mission. The most urgent task is to reduce "social distancing," step by step, meter by meter, centimeter by centimeter. The art world—and by this I mean artists, art institutions, art academies, art criticism, the art market, must not adopt "social distancing." Simply because Art is autonomous, universal, absolute, and necessary, and as such can't have any distance. I have never questioned the temporary usefulness of the toxic term "social distancing," but it must, under no circumstance, become the new paradigm for living together in the world, in the art world. It is urgent to work on it and show that Art—because it's Art—can create a dialogue or a confrontation one-to-one, at eye level. It is important to insist that Art is "resistant," which means that art resists economic, cultural, political, aesthetic facts. The question is not about ignoring the Coronavirus issue—on the contrary, it's about taking it seriously and understanding it as a warning, as a test, as a challenge. I believe that contact, encounter, exchange, neighborhood, confrontation, freedom, freedom in non-freedom, inclusivity, multiplicity, solidarity, equality, creativity are concepts that are more important than ever, because they've been challenged by the imposed "social distancing."

OUT   183

Here, the artist has a decisive role to play, since
concepts such as distance, control, social control,
containment, security, guarantee, tracing, repression,
exclusivity have nothing to do with the experience
of Art. Rather, resistance is needed to combat
opportunistic, consumerist, and exclusionary ten-
dencies—which have always existed in the art world.
My weapon will be my work—and I want to do it
with exaggerated *bienveillance.* I use the French term
bienveillance (kindness, benevolence)—*bienveillance
exagérée*—because it describes precisely what I mean.
"Exaggerated" because this crisis is exaggerated, the
response to COVID-19 is exaggerated, while—unfortunately—the consequences of the increasing loss of
primary and fundamental personal freedom are not
exaggerated; they are truly real.

I want to work with exaggerated *bienveillance*
toward the other. I want to work with exaggerated
bienveillance to the world—to our whole and only
world—and I want to work with exaggerated
bienveillance to myself. I want to learn something
from this crisis and take decisions. It's about using
Art—more than ever—as a tool to engage with the
world, to confront the time in which I live and face
the reality surrounding me. I want to confront the
precarious, the insecure, the non-guaranteed, the
uncertain, the indeterminate, the strange, the fright-
ening, the uncanny with exaggerated *bienveillance*
in my Art. I am thinking of an intelligent, generous,
dynamic, demanding, active, asserting, practical, and
combative *bienveillance*—it's not about a passive,
wait-and-see, spiritual, religious, theoretical benevolence. I want to point out what I am prepared to live
and work for—this is my mission as an artist working
today. "Social distancing" and "home office" are
not part of it. It would be a mistake to step into this
stupid and clumsy—but also tempting—trap. "Virtual
exhibitions," "virtual artworks," "virtual learning,"

"virtual exchange," "virtual communication" are only sham solutions or excuses, all the more dangerous because they are desired, encouraged, or even required by state authorities. But nobody—not even the State—can tell me how to work in the future. Therefore, it is essential to be sensitive, critical, alert, and attentive to the virtual and the digital—there is no need to hide behind the computer. We must resist the temptation of "keeping among ourselves" and "diving into the Internet"—in the art world as well. To give way to the tendency of "isolating" or "self-isolation" would mean to give up debate, discussion, criticism, conflict—everything that Art can create. That's why I question—like many others—the ongoing dogma of distancing technologies.

Art, because it's Art, is universal. Universality means Justice, Equality, the Other, Truth. We need to remain truthful to this prerequisite. We must never give up the notion of beauty. Beauty must be occupied and preserved from capitalism, from consumerism, from the fashion industry. We do not want to abandon beauty to the glamor business. Everything that is beautiful has to come from the inside, from myself, from ourselves, in confronting the world. Something beautiful arises if there is an engagement and if the mystery contained in this engagement remains. It is the autonomy and the absoluteness of the artwork that gives it its beauty.

The Way Out … into Public Space

The way out is literally the way into public space. The goals, the ambition, the mission for work in public space are to establish a new form of sculpture, in making encounters, creating an event, and to think sculpture in public space today. I believe that we must rethink Art in public space as an experience that can lead to a transformation, while keeping in mind that Art in public space is not a success nor a

failure—Art in public space, or simply Art—is never
a total success nor a total failure. Art is an event, Art
proposes an experience, an existential experience.
The "Non-Exclusive Audience" is the essential public
to conquer and reconquer. It understands and is
willing to experience that an event without transformation is not an event. It knows that transformation
can only happen because "non-satisfaction" is
experienced as "resistance." "Non-satisfaction" is a
tool to resist cultural, economic, political, and social
habits. Art in public space must be a work of art and
not a cultural event. Culture leads to satisfaction—a
satisfaction that remains passive—as opposed to Art,
which offers "non-satisfaction" and is active. I believe
that this "non-satisfaction" allows the shaping of a
new dynamic, a dynamic or a movement in which
a new form of sculpture in public space is created,
deployed, and even redeployed. It is the strong and
fragile, the beautiful and conflictual, the enlightening
and problematic affirmation of a form. It is a precarious form of friendship through the experience
"Art." Like every friendship, it is something beyond
argumentation, beyond proof, beyond guarantee.
Friendship is one of the most valuable things we can
gain in this world. Friendship's essence is loyalty, the
loyalty to Art and to its search for form, for freedom,
and for mystery.

Here I want to pay tribute to David Hammons's
understanding of Art in public space and to the work
of this artist. He said: "The art audience is the worst
audience in the world. It's overly educated, it's conservative, it's out to criticize not to understand, and
it never has any fun! Why should I spend my time
playing to that audience? That's like going into a lion's
den. So I refuse to deal with that audience and I'll
play with the street audience. That audience is more
human and their opinion is from the heart. They
don't have any reason to play games, there's nothing

gained or lost."[1] This potent quote has followed me
since I first read it. This clear way of putting forth the
complexity and beauty, but also the difficulty and
problematic nature of the endeavor of working in
public space, has encouraged and still encourages
me. David Hammons knows that Art in public space
means conflict, but also an opportunity for the artist
to give this conflict a form.

~~The Way Out of … Obsolete Institutional and Museum Practices into "The Museum of The Future"~~

The way out is the way to change what is obsolete. We
have to change obsolete Institutional and Museum
Practices; this is an absolute necessity. A lot of things
in Contemporary Art are obsolete because they
have nothing to do with art, but with fashion, with
commerce, with exclusion, with social status, with
VIP ideology. The "Non-Exclusive Audience" is a tool
against Contemporary Art's VIP ideology. I reproach
museums—in general—for not producing confrontation. I reproach museums for not believing in the
autonomy of Art, and I reproach museums for not
believing in the universality of Art. A museum must
believe and assert the intrinsic power of works of art
in establishing a direct confrontation or dialogue—
one-on-one. However, museums establish distancing:
through communication, history, and culture. Even
more so through control and Coronavirus responses.
The tendency is to try to neutralize Art through
culture. Art is accepted when it possesses a "cultural
surplus." This "cultural surplus" is a danger for the
work of art. Tools (or guidelines) to avoid "cultural
surplus" are a true and uncompromising logic
against the "exclusive audience," against everything
"exclusive" in general. The term "exclusive" is
continuously being used in art to argue, to intimidate,
and to legitimize. "Exclusivity" has become a positive

criterion. In other words, the "non-exclusive public" is the opposite of a predetermined, selected, and initiated public. The deployment of public space in the museum and in the public institution is the way out of an announced disaster. The way out needs to lead to something new. It's the way into "The Museum of the Future." It demands a clear, serious, and sober logic, the logic of Truth, of the Universal, of Justice, and of Equality. This is the logic for opening toward the "Non-Exclusive Audience." The Museum of the Future will be a place to encounter and confront art, philosophy, and poetry. It will be a museum where public space is used, thus becoming a living museum, a real living space.

The Museum of the Future's guidelines are: "Presence" and "Production." "Presence" and "Production" are a gift, an offensive gift, given to provoke other presences and other productions. This is a demanding alternative to the lazy, demagogic, and so-called democratic term "Participation." I am not for "Participative Art," because the first real participation is the participation of thinking. Participation is only another word for consumption! The artist, the philosopher, or the poet have to give something first, in order to oblige the other (the "Non-Exclusive Audience") to give something (his/her time and his/her production). This is another distinction between "Presence and Production" and "Participation." I believe that throughout "Presence" and "Production"—my production and my presence first—the Museum of the Future can create involvement, implication, exchange, dialogue, confrontation, contact!

Non-programming is another guideline of the Museum of the Future. Non-programming is new and necessary because it keeps us awake and alert. Non-programming is the assertion that art, philosophy, and poetry can create a dialogue and

 WA

confrontation unexpectedly, without a program, without a schedule. Lectures, exhibitions, discussions, films, performances can run at any time; there will be no "previews" or opening announcements. It will be possible to walk into the Museum of the Future with no set "program" or predisposition. The conditions for the Museum of the Future that I propose are free access for everyone at all times, open every day, 24/7 with no closing hours. The Museum of the Future will have no guards or security. Instead, everyone working in the Museum of the Future will consider him or herself as "first visitor," with the task of transforming the Museum. The "first visitor" must be the most interested and most implicated, the biggest lover of Art, philosophy, and poetry. This is the reason for working in the Museum of the Future. This means that instead of security, the institution is present and the first one concerned, the first to stand for Art.

The Museum of the Future has the ambition to offer a public space, to be a home or even a shelter. Therefore, no more fancy, narcissistic, and useless "museum architecture" is needed. Art does not need an "ideal" location to exist. Art can exist, will exist, must exist wherever it is, and Art definitely addresses everybody.

Paris, December 2021

1 David Hammons, interview by Kellie Jones, *Real Life Magazine* 16 (1986): pp. 2–9.

190THE   WA

Editors' Biographies

EKATERINA DEGOT (1958, Moscow, Russia) is an art historian, researcher, and curator focusing on aesthetic and sociopolitical issues in Russia and Eastern Europe from the 19th century to the post-Soviet era. She began her tenure as director and chief curator of steirischer herbst in 2018. From 2014 to 2017, Degot was artistic director of the Academy of the Arts of the World in Cologne. Among other shows, she curated the First Ural Industrial Biennial in Yekaterinburg (2010, with Cosmin Costinas and David Riff) and headed the first Bergen Assembly with David Riff (2013). Degot lives in Graz.

DAVID RIFF (1975, London, United Kingdom) is a writer, translator, artist, curator, and former member of the art group Chto Delat. He has been a curator at steirischer herbst since 2018. Among other shows, Riff cocurated the First Ural Industrial Biennial in Yekaterinburg (2010, with Cosmin Costinas and Ekaterina Degot) and headed the first Bergen Assembly together with Ekaterina Degot (2013). His most recent effort as an artist-curator was a large-scale exhibition on Mikhail Lifshitz in Moscow (2018, with Dmitry Gutov). Riff lives in Berlin.

Contributors' Biographies

KATHERINE ANGEL is an academic and writer whose 2012 work of literary nonfiction, *Unmastered: A Book on Desire, Most Difficult to Tell*, attracted worldwide attention. It was followed by *Daddy Issues* (2019) and *Tomorrow Sex Will Be Good Again: Women and Desire in the Age of Consent* (2021). Her articles have been published in magazines and journals internationally. She lives in London.

Along with many other subjects, EMMA DOWLING studies feminist political economy, emotions and work, social justice and social change, and financialization and society. She is currently assistant professor for the sociology of social change at the Department of Sociology at the University of Vienna. One of her best-known publications is *The Care Crisis: What Caused It and How Can We End It?* (2021). She lived in London for many years and currently lives in Vienna.

DOROTHEA VON HANTELMANN is a professor of art and society at Bard College Berlin. Her main fields of research are contemporary art and theory as well as the history and theory of exhibitions. Among her publications are *How to Do Things with Art* (2010) and *Die Ausstellung: Politik eines Rituals* (2012). Her current book project explores exhibitions as ritual sites from the 16th century to the present. She lives in Berlin.

THOMAS HIRSCHHORN (1957, Bern, Switzerland) is an artist famous for his installations, collages, and community projects. His installations and public works often use common everyday materials such as cardboard, foil, and duct tape, bringing together mind maps, found images, and drawings in complex arrangements. Committed to a nonexclusive relation to the public, Hirschhorn's work often reaches out to audiences excluded from contemporary art. He lives in Paris.

HIWA K (1975, Sulaymaniyah, Kurdistan Region / Iraq) is an artist whose sculptures, videos, and performances weave together his own biography with those of friends, family, and perfect strangers. Bringing difficult topics like war, migration, and the effects of neoliberalism down to earth, his work often has a participatory dimension and involves collaboration with people from all walks of life. After decades of living in Germany, Hiwa K lives in Iraq.

JASON W. MOORE teaches world history at Binghamton University, where he is professor of sociology and coordinator of the World-Ecology Research Group. He is the author or editor of several books, including *Capitalism in the Web of Life* (2015) and, with Raj Patel, *A History of the World in Seven Cheap Things* (2017). Many of his essays, translated into fifteen languages, can be found on his website: jasonwmoore.com.

EVGENY MOROZOV (1984, Soligorsk, Belarus) is a writer and researcher who studies the political and social implications of technology. Morozov's writings have appeared in various newspapers and magazines around the world. His books include *The Net Delusion: The Dark Side of Internet Freedom* (2011) and *To Save Everything, Click Here* (2013). Morozov, who holds a PhD in history of science from Harvard University, is also the initiator of *The Syllabus*, a curated Internet newsletter launched in 2019.

PAUL B. PRECIADO (1970, Burgos, Spain) is a writer, philosopher, curator, and one of the leading thinkers in the study of gender and body politics. His book *Testo Junkie* (2008) was a pioneering account of his own gender transition, where he explores the relation of technology and the construction of gender. He has been curator of public programs of Documenta 14 (Kassel/Athens), curator of the Taiwan Pavilion at the Venice Biennale in 2019, and head of research of the Museum of Contemporary Art of Barcelona (MACBA). He lives in Paris.

QUINN SLOBODIAN (1978, Edmonton, Canada) is Marion Butler MacLean Associate Professor of the History of Ideas at Wellesley College. His most recent books are *Globalists: The End of Empire and the Birth of Neoliberalism* (2018) and *Market Civilizations: Neoliberals East and West* (2022), edited with Dieter Plehwe. His next book, on capitalist exit fantasies, will appear in 2023. He lives in Cambridge, MA.

MARK TERKESSIDIS (1966, Eschweiler, Germany) is a journalist, migration researcher, and author of numerous articles and books on racism, migration, and youth and pop culture. His publications include, *Interkultur* (2010), *Kollaboration* (2015), *Nach der Flucht: Neue Ideen für die Einwanderungs- gesellschaft* (2017), and *Wessen Erinnerung zählt? Koloniale Vergangenheit und Rassismus heute* (2019). He lives in Berlin.

Energy Sponsor

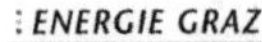

Exhibition Sponsor

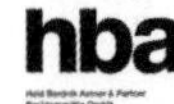

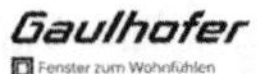

Technical Sponsor Helmut List Halle

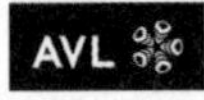

Project Supporters

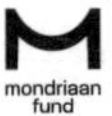

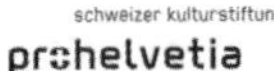

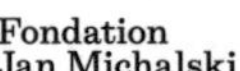

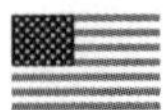

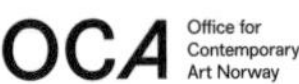

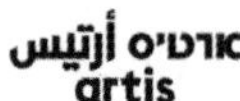

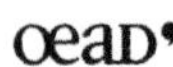

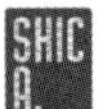

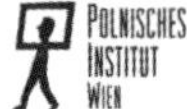

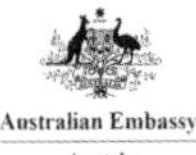

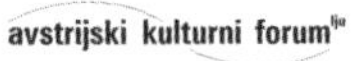

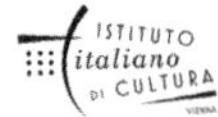

Project Supporters

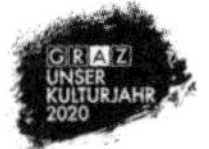

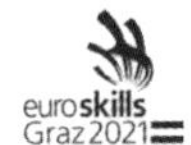

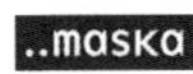

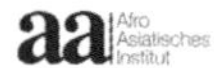

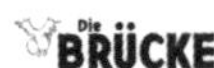

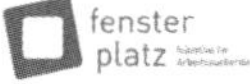

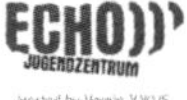

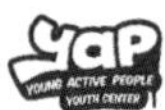

**steirischer herbst '21
Festival Team**

Ekaterina Degot
Director and Chief Curator

Henriette Gallus
Deputy Director

Christoph Platz
Head of Curatorial Affairs

Rita Puffer
Chief Financial Officer

Carina Hutter
Management Assistant /
Coordinator National Project
Funding and Protocol Events

Theresa Weiler
Management Assistant

David Riff
Senior Curator

Mirela Baciak
Curator

Dominik Müller
Curator

Džana Ajanović
Curatorial Assistant

Barbara Seyerl
Research Assistant / University
Program Coordinator

Hannes Bemm
Coordinator Sponsorship, Media
Partners, and International
Project Funding

Judith Brand
Press and Public Relations Officer

Arash Shahali
International Media Adviser

Vesna Pajičić
Coordinator Visitors' Service

Christina Kasic
Assistant Communications
and Protocol Events

Assistants Communication
Alina Radkovic
Theresa Neureiter
Eva Triebl
Lisa Wonnebauer

Sedra Arab
Communications Intern

Martina Heil
Editorial Coordinator /
Coordinator Communications

Jeff Thoss
Managing Editor

Fotini Lazaridou-Hatzigoga
Website Manager

Dietmar Reinbacher
Head of herbst Education

Johannes Leitich
Head of herbst Education
(until October 2021)

Lena Riecnik
Coordinator herbst Education

Ajda Goznik
herbst Education for Apprentices

Markus Plasencia
herbst Education for Schools

Jakob Schweighofer
Senior Production Manager

Sebastian Sprenger
Production Manager

Roland Gfrerer
Production Manager

Jacqueline Emathinger
Coordinator Production Office

Karl Masten
Technical Management

Johanna Arco
Project Coordinator

Project Coordinators
Shirin Hooshmandi
Lukas Kaiser
Heinz Leitner
Marcel Masten
Nicolas Müller-Lorenz
Maria-Oscara Ohrenstein
Martin Pelzmann
Ronny Priesching
Eva Schmartschan
Guggi Schneider
Andreas Schögler
Lisa Schöttel
Lena Truppe

Marlene Obermayer
Head of Archive/Library

Stefanie Lazarus
Office Management

Matthias Ulbl
Accounting

Kathrin Lazarus
Coordinator Human Resources
and Archive Assistant

Simon Resch
Office Assistant

Danica Radat
Facility Manager

Grupa Ee (Mina Fina, Damjan
Ilić, Ivian Kan Mujezinović)
Graphic Design

Systemantics
Website

Colophon

This book is published in conjunction with steirischer herbst festival steirischer herbst '21—*The Way Out*, September 9–October 10, 2021, Graz, Styria, Austria.

This edition of steirischer herbst was created by all participating artists, partner institutions, thinkers, philosophers, as well as Ekaterina Degot, Director and Chief Curator, Henriette Gallus, Deputy Director, Christoph Platz, Head of Curatorial Affairs, David Riff, Senior Curator, Dominik Müller, Curator, Mirela Baciak, Curator, and the steirischer herbst team.

Editors:
Ekaterina Degot
David Riff

With contributions by:
Katherine Angel, Emma Dowling, Dorothea von Hantelmann, Thomas Hirschhorn, Hiwa K, Jason W. Moore, Evgeny Morozov, Paul B. Preciado, Quinn Slobodian, Mark Terkessidis

Project management:
Henriette Gallus, steirischer herbst
Fabian Reichel, Hatje Cantz

Managing editor:
Jeff Thoss

Copyediting:
Melissa Larner

Proofreading:
Aaron Bogart

Graphic design:
Grupa Ee (Mina Fina, Damjan Ilić, Ivian Kan Mujezinović)

steirischer herbst festival gmbh
Sackstraße 17
8010 Graz, Austria
www.steirischerherbst.at

Production:
Vinzenz Geppert, Hatje Cantz

Printing:
DZS Grafik

Paper:
Munken Print White 1.5, 90 g/m²

© 2022 Hatje Cantz Verlag, Berlin, steirischer herbst, Graz, and authors

Published by
Hatje Cantz Verlag GmbH
Mommsenstraße 27
10629 Berlin
www.hatjecantz.com
A Ganske Publishing Group Company

ISBN 978-3-7757-5366-1

Printed in Slovenia

Cover illustration:
Grupa Ee

Every effort has been made to trace the copyright holders and obtain permission to reproduce material. Please do get in touch with any enquiries or any information relating to unintended omissions.